Goldwin Smith

Does the Bible Sanction American Slavery?

Goldwin Smith

Does the Bible Sanction American Slavery?

ISBN/EAN: 9783744793773

Printed in Europe, USA, Canada, Australia, Japan

Cover: Foto ©Lupo / pixelio.de

More available books at **www.hansebooks.com**

DOES THE BIBLE SANCTION AMERICAN SLAVERY?

BY

GOLDWIN SMITH.

Oxford and London:
JOHN HENRY AND JAMES PARKER.
1863.

PREFACE.

THE following pages are an expansion of a lecture delivered at the Manchester Athenæum, and the author has to plead as his justification for printing them, the wishes of some of his audience on that occasion.

They treat of the subject stated on the title-page; not of the justice or wisdom of the present war, nor of the conduct of any American party.

The argument is as much historical as theological: and the question whether the Book, which Christendom regards as the rule of conduct, is favourable to Slavery or to Free Labour, to the degradation or to the independence and dignity of the labouring class, is interesting to the statesman and economist as well as to the divine.

It will be remembered that we have no longer to deal with the question between immediate and gradual emancipation, as to which the greatest enemies of Slavery may fairly differ; nor with the excuses which may be made for those who have inherited a bad system not of their own creating, and which no reasonable man would desire to withhold. A complete change has of late taken place in the sentiments and language of the Southern States on the subject of Slavery. That which was regarded and spoken of by Washington and the statesmen of his time as a transient evil, is now declared to be a permanent good, and not only a permanent good, but the best of all social institutions. Mr. Stephens, the Vice-President of the Slave States, avows that "the foundations of the new Government are laid upon the great truth, that Slavery—subordination to the superior race—is the Negro's natural and moral condition; that it is the first Government in the history of the world based upon this great physical, philosophical, and moral truth; and that the stone which was rejected by the first builders is in the new edifice become the chief stone of the corner." Those who hold and proclaim such sentiments as these may naturally proceed to still more extensive and startling doctrines affecting the position of the labourer, without regard to the colour of his skin, in all the countries of the world.

With regard to the part of the argument turning upon the Laws of Moses, Michaelis has long since made us familiar with the fact that these

Laws were not a new Code, but a revision of the old customary law of the nation. But since his time much light has been thrown upon this subject by eminent writers on the philosophy of history and on the history of the Jews.

Many of the points here mentioned have been mentioned before in various works; but the author is not aware that the question has been placed as a whole exactly in the light in which he wished and has here endeavoured to place it.

In this discussion the authority of the Pentateuch is taken for granted on both sides. In using, therefore, the common language on the subject, the author is not presuming to pass any opinion upon the questions respecting the date and authorship of the Books which divide great Hebraists and theologians, and which, he is perfectly aware, can be decided only by free inquiry, carried on by men learned in the subject, with absolute faith in the God of Truth.

DOES THE BIBLE SANCTION AMERICAN SLAVERY?

WHEN a New World was peopled, strange things were sure to be seen. And strange things are seen in America. By the side of the Great Salt Lake is a community basing itself upon Polygamy. In the Southern States is a community basing itself upon Slavery. Each of these communities confidently appeals to the Bible as its sanction; and each of them, in virtue of that warrant, declares its peculiar institution to be universal and divine. The plea of the slave-owner is accepted. Perhaps if the Mormonite were equally an object of political interest to a large party, his plea might be accepted also [a].

It is important in more ways than one to determine whether the slave-owner's plea is true. The character of the Bible is threatened; and so is the character of the English law and nation. *The Times* says that slavery is only wrong as luxury is wrong, and that the Bible

[a] No less a person than Luther was in fact led, by his irrational treatment of the Bible, into both errors. He preached the doctrine that a slave had no right to escape even from a heathen master, (see his *Heer-Predigt wider die Türken*,) and he brought an eternal scandal on Protestantism by sanctioning the double marriage of the Elector of Hesse.

B

enjoins the slave at the present day to return to his master. If so, the law of England, which takes away the slave from his master directly his feet touch English soil, is a robber's law. If so, the great Act of Emancipation, of which we speak so proudly, was a robber's act; for though a partial compensation for their loss was granted to the West Indian slave-owners, they were forced to give up their slaves notoriously against their will.

SECTION I.

It is true that the Old Testament distinctly recognises Slavery as a Hebrew institution. It is also true that the New Testament speaks of Slavery in several passages and does not condemn it.

But before we draw the conclusion that Slavery is a divine institution established by God for all time, we must consider what was the object of God's dealings with Man recorded in the Bible.

If it was to put human society at once in a state of perfection, without further effort, political, social or intellectual, on the part of Man, the inference is irresistible that every institution enjoined in the Bible is part of a perfect scheme, and that every institution mentioned in the Bible without condemnation will be lawful to the end of time.

But if the object was to implant in man's heart a principle, viz. the love of God and Man, which should move him to work (God also working in him) for the improvement of his own state and that of his fellows, and for the transforming of his and their life into the image of their Maker; in this case, it will by no means follow that any social institution recognised in Scripture for the time being, or mentioned by it without condemnation, is for ever good or lawful in the sight of God.

And that this, not the other, was the real object is matter of hourly experience; for man labours till now to improve his state and that of his fellows; and his conscience, which is the voice of God, tells him that he does well.

To say that the Bible has nothing to do with politics or science, is a bad way of escaping from a difficulty of our own creating. The Bible has much to do with politics and science, and with everything that enters, as all parts of our social and intellectual state do enter, into the moral life of man. But it does not suddenly reveal political and scientific truth without calling for any effort on the part of man himself to attain them; because such a revelation, instead of promoting, would have defeated the end for which, as the voice of our free moral nature assures us, the world was made. It implants in man the principle which leads him to good action of every kind. The love of God and Man, moving to disinterested efforts for the good of the community, is the source of all political improvement, at least of all that is real and lasting. And the same affection moves the high and self-devoted labours which have led to the discovery of scientific and philosophic truth. And thus in its onward progress human nature is by the very condition of that progress changed into the likeness of its Maker. Why God should choose gradual improvement rather than immediate perfection, this is not the place to inquire. That He does so, appears from the history not only of the moral, but of the physical world.

The Bible recognises Progress. The New Testament says of the Old Testament that Moses gave the Jews certain things for the hardness of their hearts; not, of course, for their wickedness, to which God would not bend His law, but for their rude and uncivilized state. And not merely for their rudeness and want of civilization, but for the primitive narrowness of the circle of their affections: for it is only in the course of history, and with the increasing range of man's social vision, that his affection extends from the primæval family to the tribe, from the tribe to the nation, and from the nation to mankind. And as to the New Testament itself, it breathes in every page boundless hope for the future, together with the charity which is the source of social effort, and with the faith which carries each man beyond the sensual objects of his own short life. And it closes with that splendid vision of the consummation of all Christian effort in the perfect reign of God on earth, from which folly attempts to cast, like an astrologer, the horoscope of nations; but which is in truth the last voice of Christianity, as it passes from the hands of the Apostles and commits itself to the dark and dangerous tide of human affairs, breaking forth in the assurance of final victory.

The true spiritual life of the world commenced in the Chosen People. He who denies this would seem to deny not a theory of Inspiration, but a great and manifest fact of history. But the spiritual life commenced under an earthly mould of national life similar in all respects, political, social and literary, to those of other races. The Jewish nation, in short, was a nation, not a miracle. Had it been a miracle, it might have shewn forth the power of God, like the stars in heaven, but it would have been nothing to the rest of mankind, nor could its spiritual life have helped to awaken theirs [b].

This commencement of the spiritual life was marked by the appearance (1) of a Cosmogony which, unlike those of heathen nations, gave a true account of the origin of the world and of Man, and a true account of the relations between Man and his Creator; (2) of a series of histories written on a moral and religious principle, and still unrivalled among historical writings for the steadiness with which this, the true key to history, is kept in view; (3) of a body of religious literature, in the shape of hymns, reflections, preachings, apologues, which though not Christian, and therefore not to be indiscriminately used by Christians, was wholly unapproached among the heathen; (4) of a Code of Laws the beneficence of which is equally unapproached by any code, and least of all by any Oriental code, not produced under the influence of Christianity.

This code of laws takes the rude institutions of a primitive nation, including Slavery, as they stand,

[b] See the Author's work on *Rational Religion*, p. 50.

not changing society by miracle, which, as has been said before, seems to have been no part of the purposes of God. But while it takes these institutions as they stand, it does not perpetuate them, but reforms them, mitigates them, and lays on them restrictions tending to their gradual abolition. Much less does it introduce any barbarous institution or custom for the first time.

To shew that this principle is not invented for the case of Slavery, we will try to verify it in some other cases first. It will be the more worth while to do this, because if the principle be sound, it may help to relieve the distress caused by doubts as to the morality of the Old Testament on other points as well as on the question now in issue. It may do this at a less expense than that of supposing the existence of two different Moralities, one for God, the other for Man, and thus making Man worship, what to his mind must be, an immoral God.

In times before the reign of Law, justice was done on the murderer by the nearest kinsman of the murdered as Avenger of Blood. Such justice was a degree better than no justice; and a custom which assigned the sacred duty of revenge to a particular person, instead of leaving it to any chance hand, was the first step towards the appointment of a regular magistrate. This institution seems to have been universal among primitive tribes. A relic of it lingered in the law of this country till the reign of George III., when Wager of Battle having been demanded in a case of murder by the nearest of kin against the murderer, as a common law right, the demand was with difficulty evaded.

The law of Moses accordingly recognises the Avenger of Blood, (Numb. xxxv., &c.)

But the custom was liable to great abuses, which were apt to make it a step backwards instead of forwards in morality and civilization. (1.) The same revenge was taken for blood however shed, whether wilfully or accidentally, which confounded men's notion of crime, and in fact multiplied murders. (2.) When covetousness overcame revenge, and the slain kinsman was not very dear, a sum of money (called by our German ancestors the *wehrgeld*) was taken for his blood instead of the blood of the slayer; and this practice grew into a regular system, which destroyed the distinction between crime and civil injury, took away the sanctity of human life, the foundation-stone of civilization, and moreover sharpened barbarous divisions of class, since the price of a man's blood was assessed in the tariff according to his rank. (3.) Revenge became hereditary, and blood feuds arose between family and family or clan and clan, which filled the world with slaughter. Such blood feuds were common in the Highlands while the old clans existed, and they are still common among the wild tribes of Syria and in other parts of the East.

Now (1) the law of Moses expressly distinguishes wilful murder from accidental homicide, and confines the office of the Avenger of Blood to wilful murder. "And if he smite him with an instrument of iron, so that he die, he is a murderer: the murderer shall surely be put to death. . . . Or if he smite him with a hand weapon of wood, wherewith he may die, and he die, he is a murderer: the murderer shall surely be put to death. The revenger of blood himself shall slay the murderer: when he meeteth him, he shall slay him. But if he thrust him of hatred, or hurl at him by laying of wait, that he die; or in enmity smite him with his hand, that he die: he that smote him shall surely be put to death; for he is a murderer: the revenger of blood shall slay the murderer, when he meeteth him. But if he thrust him suddenly without enmity, or have cast upon him anything without laying of wait, or with any stone, wherewith a man may die, seeing him not, and cast it upon him, that he die, and was not his enemy, neither sought his harm: then the congregation shall judge between the slayer and the revenger of blood according to these judgments: and the congregation shall deliver the slayer out of the hand of the revenger of blood, and the congregation shall restore him to the city of his refuge, whither he was fled: and he shall abide in it unto the death of the high priest, which was anointed with the holy oil[c]." (2.) The taking of money as a satisfaction for blood is strictly forbidden. "Ye shall take no satisfaction for the life of a murderer which is guilty of death: but he shall be surely put to death. And ye shall take no satisfaction for him that is fled to the city of his refuge, that he should come again to dwell in the land, until the death of the priest[d]." (3.) Hereditary blood feuds are forbidden with equal strictness[e]. "The fathers shall not be put to death for the children, neither shall the children be

---

[c] Numb. xxx. 16—25.   [d] Ibid., v. 31, 32.
[e] Deut. xxiv. 16.

put to death for the fathers: every man shall be put to death for his own sin."

By providing judges in all the tribes to do equal justice between man and man[f], and by calling the congregation to judge between the slayer and the avenger of blood[g], Moses secures the speedy departure of the need of private revenge and the speedy advent of a reign of public law.

The right of *Asylum* is another primitive institution which is recognised by the Law of Moses; and which was not without use in its day, as the history of the Middle Ages, no less than that of the more ancient barbarism, can bear witness. It gave vengeance time for reflection, and in default of a magistrate armed with sufficient powers, helped to prevent society from becoming a slaughter-house. But this institution also was liable to the grossest abuses. It sheltered the wilful murderer as well as him who had killed a man accidentally or in self-defence, and in the case of wilful murder led to a final defeat of justice. Being connected with holy places and the priests who kept them, it bred gross superstition. For the same reason, and because the asylum was a source of power and profit to the priests, asylums were multiplied till they gave impunity to crime. In the reign of Tiberius the Roman Government found it necessary to interfere with the growing license of setting up asylums in the Greek cities of the Empire. "The temples were filled with the vilest of the slaves; the same receptacles sheltered

[f] Deut. i. 16.   [g] Numb. xxxv. 24.

debtors from their creditors and persons suspected of capital offences from justice. And authority was unable to restrain the fanatical violence of the people, who protected the crimes of men as a part of the worship of the Gods."

Here, too, the Mosaic law abstains from abolishing the custom, which could not have been done without antedating the progress of society and taking man out of his own hands; but it guards against the abuse. The cities of refuge were not to be for the wilful murderer, but "that the slayer may flee thither which killeth any person *at unawares*[h]." "These six cities shall be a refuge, both for the children of Israel, and for the stranger, and for the sojourner among them: that every one that killeth any person *unawares* may flee thither[i]." The number of the places of refuge is strictly limited to six; and they are to be cities, not holy places to which any superstition could attach. Further to guard against such superstition, it is expressly declared that the holiest of all holy places shall not shelter the criminal. "But if a man come presumptuously upon his neighbour, to slay him with guile; thou shalt take him *from Mine altar*, that he may die[k]."

In other nations of antiquity, and in Europe during the Middle Ages, the fugitive had to take up his abode for life in the asylum or sanctuary; at least he could never leave it with safety: and thus these places became nests of crime, as the neighbourhoods of some of them, Westminster for instance, are at the present day.

[h] Numb. xxxv. 11.   [i] Ib. 15.   [k] Exod. xxi. 14.

The Hebrew Law guards against this by providing that the fugitive shall be required to remain in the city of refuge only till the death of the high priest, after which he may leave it with impunity. "If the slayer shall at any time come without the border of the city of his refuge, whither he was fled; and the revenger of blood find him without the borders of the city of his refuge, and the revenger of blood kill the slayer; he shall not be guilty of blood: because he should have remained in the city of his refuge until the death of the high priest: but after the death of the high priest the slayer shall return into the land of his possession [1]."

Again, in Patriarchal times, the family being the State, and the only government being that of the father of the family, the father, as supreme ruler, had the power of life and death over his child. Among the Romans, tenacious of all old institutions and full of the lust of dominion abroad and at home, this power, under the name of *patria potestas,* was retained long after the state of society by which alone it was justified had passed away. It remained a hideous and disgraceful relic of barbarism amidst the meridian light of Roman jurisprudence; and Erixon, a Roman knight, put his son to death in the time of Seneca. The power extended over the wife as well as over the child. It was exercised by the Roman father arbitrarily and privately; so that till public feeling at last put it down, there was no check on it whatever.

Now the law of Moses, coming at a time when a national government had not been completely formed,

[1] Numb. xxxv. 26—28.

and the family had not yet been completely brought under the State, abstains from directly abolishing the father's power; but it places it under restrictions which amount as nearly as possible to abolition. "If a man have a stubborn and rebellious son, which will not obey the voice of his father or the voice of his mother, and that, when they have chastened him, will not hearken unto them: then shall his father and his mother lay hold on him, and bring him out unto the elders of his city and unto the gate of his place; and they shall say unto the elders of his city, This our son is stubborn and rebellious, he will not obey our voice; he is a glutton and a drunkard. And all the men of his city shall stone him with stones, that he die: so shalt thou put evil away from among you; and all Israel shall hear and fear." Here, we see, (1) the concurrence of the mother as well as of the father in the death of the child, (2) a definite charge, and (3) a public proceeding before a solemn tribunal are required. It may safely be said that a power so limited would not be abused.

So, too, *Polygamy* prevailed in primitive times: and in those times there might be a ground for it. When there was no government or law to protect the weak, a woman was absolutely dependent on the protection of a husband or a son, and if she had remained unmarried she would have been the helpless prey of violence and lust. Not only so, but, when the family was all in all, she would have been a miserable outcast on the face of the earth. And, as usual, sentiment accommodated itself to the state of society: so that affection was not wounded, nor the dignity of woman degraded, by a double marriage. Leah and Rachel are, and would necessarily be, as unconscious of impurity and therefore in soul as pure, as two daughters of one father. It did not follow that men were never to rise from the lower state of 'society into the higher; or that a relapse into polygamy, now that woman needs no protection but that of the law, and has become conscious of her due position, would be anything but brutality and crime.

The Hebrew lawgiver could not have forbidden polygamy without changing the state of society by a miracle, or breeding confusion, and doing a wrong in some cases to woman. But he does not perpetuate or encourage it: he recognises it only to mitigate its evils. "If a man have two wives, one beloved, and another hated, and they have born him children, both the beloved and the hated; and if the firstborn son be hers that was hated: then it shall be, when he maketh his sons to inherit that which he hath, that he may not make the son of the beloved firstborn before the son of the hated, which is indeed the firstborn; but he shall acknowledge the son of the hated for the firstborn, by giving him a double portion of all that he hath: for he is the beginning of his strength; the right of the firstborn is his [m]."

Shall we say, then, with these things before us, that the Bible sanctions Private Revenge, the right of Asylum for criminals, the exercise of a power of life and death by parents over their children, or the practice of Polygamy; that it establishes these as

[m] Deut. xxi. 15—17.

divine institutions intended for all time; and enjoins the revival of them, where they have been allowed to fall out of use, in civilized and Christian lands?

The Mosaic laws of war for the present day would be very inhuman: for that day, and compared with the practices blazoned on the triumphal monuments of Assyrian and Egyptian warriors, they were humane. "When thou comest nigh unto a city to fight against it, then proclaim peace unto it. And it shall be, if it make thee answer of peace and open unto thee, then it shall be, that all the people that is found therein shall be tributaries unto thee, and they shall serve thee. And if it will make no peace with thee, but will make war against thee, then thou shalt besiege it; and when the Lord thy God hath delivered it into thine hands, thou shalt smite every male thereof with the edge of the sword: but the women, and the little ones, and the cattle, and all that is in the city, even all the spoil thereof, shalt thou take unto thyself; and thou shalt eat the spoil of thine enemies, which the Lord thy God hath given thee[n]." That which is of Moses and of God in this passage is the command to proclaim peace to a city, and give its garrison the option of saving their lives by becoming tributaries before proceeding to the usual extremities of Oriental war. The duty of giving quarter to the garrison of a city taken by storm was not known to the group of primitive nations of which the Jews were one; it was not known to the polished Athenian who massacred the inhabitants of Melos without mercy; it was not known to the

[n] Deut. xx. 10.

combatants in the Thirty Years' War; it was hardly known to Cromwell; but it is known now.

The Greek, when he invaded a country, not only wasted the harvests of the year, but cut down the fruit-trees, which were the permanent wealth of the land. It was a common threat to an enemy, that "his cicadas should chirp upon the ground." The precept of Moses is, "When thou shalt besiege a city a long time, in making war against it to take it, thou shalt not destroy the trees thereof by forcing an axe against them; for thou mayest eat of them, and thou shalt not cut them down (for the tree of the field is man's life) to employ them in the siege: only the trees which thou knowest that they be not trees for meat, thou shalt destroy and cut them down; and thou shalt build bulwarks against the city that maketh war with thee, until it be subdued."

The heroes of Homer drag at once to their bed the unhappy woman whose city has been stormed, and whose kinsmen have been slaughtered before her eyes; and the female captives of Achilles dare not let their tears flow except under cover of a feigned mourning for Patroclus. Nor did the captive retain any personal rights: she was just as the rest of the booty, and became the absolute slave of the victor's lust. But the Hebrew law (Deut. xxi. 10,) says, "When thou goest forth to war against thine enemies, and the Lord thy God hath delivered them into thine hands, and thou hast taken them captive, and seest among the captives a beautiful woman, and hast a desire unto her, that thou wouldest have her to thy wife; then thou shalt bring her home to thine house; and she shall shave her head, and pare her nails; and she shall put the raiment of her captivity from off her, and shall remain in thine house, and bewail her father and her mother a full month: and after that thou shalt go in unto her, and be her husband, and she shall be thy wife. And it shall be, if thou have no delight in her, then thou shalt let her go whither she will; but thou shalt not sell her at all for money, thou shalt not make merchandise of her, because thou hast humbled her." Will this passage of Scripture be quoted as permitting the captors of cities in modern times to force the captured women to become their concubines?

And so as to war generally. War was the universal state of nations in early times; and the strong though coarse foundations of human character were laid in the qualities of the warrior. The Jews were always surrounded and always threatened by war. Therefore to fight valiantly for his country and his Temple was part not only of the civil duty but of the moral training of a Jew, and to be with the people in the hour of battle and exhort them to behave bravely was part of the office of the priest, and consistent with the character of his calling. "When thou goest out to battle against thine enemies, and seest horses and chariots and a people more than thou, be not afraid of them: for the Lord thy God is with thee which brought thee up out of the land of Egypt. And it shall be, when ye are come nigh unto the battle, that the priest shall approach and speak unto the people, and shall say unto them, Hear, O Israel, ye approach this day unto battle against your enemies: let not your hearts faint, fear not and do not tremble, neither be ye terrified because of them; for the Lord your God is He that goeth with you, to fight for you against your enemies to save you."

On the other hand, there is no exaltation of war above other callings, or of the military character above all other characters, such as we find in Greece, at Rome, and in the other heathen nations. There is none of that false estimate of moral qualities which produced the institutions of Sparta, and which partly leads Plato, in his ideal Republic, to propose that woman shall be trained to take part equally with man in the work of war. There are no provisions for triumphs or other military rewards; no incentives to military ambition; no rules for military education. No heaven is opened, as in the Koran, to those who fight bravely for the true God. "Peace in all your borders" is the blessing, though war is not a crime. And military pride, instead of being nursed, is rebuked by the words of the passage last quoted, which bids the Israelite put his trust, in the hour of battle, not in his own might, but in the presence of the Lord his God.

Not only so, but wars of conquest are made almost impossible by the law forbidding forced service, the means by which the great armies of the East are raised. This law follows immediately upon the passage last quoted. "And the officers shall speak unto the people, saying, What man is there that hath built a new house, and hath not dedicated it? let him go and return to his house, lest he die in the battle, and another man dedicate it. And what man is he that hath planted a vineyard, and hath not yet eaten of it? let him also go and return unto his house, lest he die in the battle, and another man eat of it. And what man is there that hath betrothed a wife, and hath not taken her? let him go and return unto his house, lest he die in the battle, and another man take her. And the officers shall speak further unto the people, and they shall say, What man is there that is fearful and fainthearted? let him go and return unto his house, lest his brethren's heart faint as well as his heart. And it shall be, when the officers have made an end of speaking unto the people, that they shall make captains of the armies to lead the people º." Pythius, a wealthy Phrygian, having gained the favour of Xerxes by the offer of a vast contribution towards the expense of the expedition against Greece, ventured to prefer a prayer to the great King. His five sons were all about to serve in the invading army; his prayer was that the eldest of them might be left behind as a stay to his own declining years, and that the service of the remaining four might be held sufficient. The King immediately ordered the eldest son of Pythius to be put to death, his body to be cut in two, and one half to be fixed on the right hand, the other on the left, on the road on which the army was to pass ᴾ.

We see also that "the captains of the armies to lead the people" are not to be made till the people are actually in the field; so that there would be no military caste or profession always burning to go to war.

The God of the Hebrews, then, is not character-

º Deut. xx. 5—9.   ᴾ Herod., ii. 210; Grote, vol. v. p. 35.

istically "a God of Battles." Compared with the Gods of the other nations He is a God of Peace. Yet He has been taken for a God of Battles, as well as for a God of Slavery, and His name has been invoked in unjust and fanatical wars.

To turn to politics. Monarchy of the Eastern sort is a barbarous form of government. Moses does not wish the Jews to adopt it: he wishes them to remain content with their free local government, the great men who would be raised up to them in time of need, their religious unity as a nation, and the monarchy of God. But all the nations around had kings, in whose hands the national strength was gathered for the purposes of war: and the people of Moses had known no political aspirations not to be abandoned without treason to their nobler nature; they had inherited no birthright of ordered freedom, the fruit of political effort through the past generations, not to be betrayed without treason to the future. There was nothing immoral in the institution, though it was better to remain without it. Therefore the lawgiver recognises it as one which might be, and was likely to be, adopted, and sets himself to guard against the evils which waited on monarchy in other Eastern nations. "When thou art come unto the land which the Lord thy God giveth thee, and shalt possess it, and shalt dwell therein, and shalt say, I will set a king over me, like as all the nations that are about me; thou shalt in any wise set him king over thee, whom the Lord thy God shall choose: one from among thy brethren shalt thou set king over thee: thou mayest not set

a stranger over thee, which is not thy brother. But
he shall not multiply horses to himself, nor cause the
people to return to Egypt, to the end that he should
multiply horses: forasmuch as the Lord hath said unto
you, Ye shall henceforth return no more that way.
Neither shall he multiply wives to himself, that his
heart turn not away: neither shall he greatly multiply
to himself silver and gold. And it shall be, when he
sitteth upon the throne of his kingdom, that he shall
write him a copy of this law in a book out of that
which is before the priests the Levites: and it shall
be with him, and he shall read therein all the days of
his life: that he may learn to fear the Lord his God,
to keep all the words of this law and these statutes, to
do them: that his heart be not lifted up above his
brethren, and that he turn not aside from the com-
mandment, to the right hand, or to the left: to the
end that he may prolong his days in his kingdom, he,
and his children, in the midst of Israel[q]." The king
of Israel is to reign by the will of God and the choice
of the people, not like a king of the Medes and Persians
by the right of his birth and the sacredness of his line:
he is to be, not a human God like the monarchs on
Egyptian and Assyrian monuments, but a man among
his brethren, and his heart is not to be lifted up above
them: unlike the neighbouring despots, he is to be be-
neath the law, which he is to study and keep, and upon
his keeping which the continuance of his reign is to
depend. Let this picture of a king be compared with
the Oriental despotism of Nebuchadnezzar and Cam-

[q] Deut. xvii. 14—20.

byses, or even with that more artificial tyranny of the Roman Emperors which has formed a model for the present government of France. Moreover, the king of Israel is not to debase himself by the lusts of the harem; nor to tax his people in order to lay up a great treasure; and he is strictly forbidden to multiply horses and chariots, which were the great instruments of aggressive war, the game of kings and the scourge of nations.

Now suppose the President of the Southern States were to make himself a king, with the powers of an Eastern monarch, could he with justice plead the Scripture as establishing monarchy and calling on the people to submit to it as a divine and universal institution?

We might apply the principle to things nearer the sanctuary. It was the custom of all primitive nations to set apart certain families or a certain tribe for religious functions; without which, before letters, or before the general use of them, there could scarcely be any certainty or stability of religion. The priest caste of Egypt, the Brachmans, the Chaldees, the hereditary guilds which kept up the worship of certain Gods in ancient Greece and Italy, were instances of the kind. But this separation had a tendency to produce caste with all its hateful and pestilential incidents. Probably there is nothing more depraved or odious in the whole range of human aberrations than the relations between the Brachmans and the Sudras as set forth in the Hindoo laws.

The Hebrew lawgiver sets apart the tribe of Levi to

keep up the religion and ritual of the nation: but in the very act of setting it apart he takes care that it shall not be a caste. "And the Lord spake unto Moses, saying, Take the Levites from among the children of Israel, and cleanse them. And thus shalt thou do unto them, to cleanse them: Sprinkle water of purifying upon them, and let them shave all their flesh, and let them wash their clothes, and so make themselves clean. Then let them take a young bullock with his meat offering, even fine flour mingled with oil, and another young bullock shalt thou take for a sin offering. And thou shalt bring the Levites before the tabernacle of the congregation: and *thou shalt gather the whole assembly of the children of Israel together:* and thou shalt bring the Levites before the Lord: and *the children of Israel shall put their hands upon the Levites:* and Aaron shall offer the Levites before the Lord *for an offering of the children of Israel,* that they may execute the service of the Lord[r]." Thus the sacred tribe is ordained to its office by the laying on of the hands of the whole people. Nor is there any restriction of religious knowledge and teaching to the Levite, as there is to the Brachmans and other priestly castes. The performance of the ritual alone is confined to the hereditary priesthood: the spiritual life of the nation is left free, and it finds its organs in the prophet and the psalmist, not in the priest.

Yet an argument has been sought in the ordinances of the Old Law concerning the Levites for the establishment in the Church of Christ of a priestly Order, self-

[r] Numb. viii. 5—11.

ordained, and invested not only with the exclusive right of performing public worship, but with the sole custody of religious truth.

So with regard to the nature of the Jewish worship. All the nations worshipped God by sacrifice and through outward forms till the mind of man had been raised high enough to worship in spirit and in truth. The Hebrew lawgiver did not originate sacrificial rites; but he elevated and purified them, and guarded them against the most horrible aberrations as to the nature of God and the mode of winning His favour and averting His wrath; as all who know the history of heathen sacrifices, Eastern or Western, must perceive. The scape-goat has been and is a subject of much mockery to philosophers. Moses did not introduce that symbolic way of relieving the souls of a people from the burden of sin and assuring them of the mercy of God: but he took care that the scape-goat should be a *goat*, and not, as at polished Athens and civilized Rome, a *man*.

The religious system of the Jews was primitive, and therefore gross compared with Christian worship. It was spiritual compared with the religious system of the most refined and cultivated heathen nations. Nevertheless, to those who did not consider it in this comparative point of view, or with reference to the time of its institution, it has supplied arguments for introducing unspiritual forms, and something resembling sacrifice, into Christian worship.

It has been said by enemies of the Bible, with some exaggeration, but also unfortunately with some truth, that modern fanatics " feed their pride on the language of the Chosen people." This is another case of the same kind. In ancient times, before Humanity was one, each nation was the "Chosen people" of a God of its own: but the Hebrew nation was the Chosen people of the true God. And as the Chosen people of the true God, the Jews were taught, compared with other nations, not national pride but national humility. They were taught, not that they had sprung of a divine seed and won their land by their own might and valour, but that "a Syrian ready to perish was their father;" that they had been bondsmen in the land of Egypt; and that they had been brought out of their bondage, not by their own arm but by the arm of their God, to Whom they owed their land and all they had. "And now, Israel, what doth the Lord thy God require of thee, but to fear the Lord thy God, to walk in all His ways, and to love Him, and to serve the Lord thy God with all thy heart and with all thy soul, to keep the commandments of the Lord, and His statutes, which I command thee this day for thy good? Behold, the heaven and the heaven of heavens is the Lord's thy God, the earth also, with all that therein is. Only the Lord had a delight in thy fathers to love them, and He chose their seed after them, even you above all people, as it is this day. Circumcise therefore the foreskin of your heart, and be no more stiff-necked. For the Lord your God is God of gods, and Lord of lords, a great God, a mighty, and a terrible, which regardeth not persons, nor taketh reward: He doth execute the judgment of the fatherless and widow, and loveth the stranger, in giving him food and raiment. Love ye therefore the stranger: for ye were strangers in the land of Egypt. Thou shalt fear the Lord thy God; Him shalt thou serve, and to Him shalt thou cleave, and swear by His Name. He is thy praise, and He is thy God, that hath done for thee these great and terrible things, which thine eyes have seen. Thy fathers went down into Egypt with three score and ten persons; and now the Lord thy God hath made thee as the stars of heaven for multitude[s]." This, though the language of a "Chosen People," is, compared with the self-praise of the Greeks and Romans, far from being the language of national pride. Yet there are some expressions in the passage which could not be used without fanaticism, by any nation or community, now that we know the relation in which all men alike stand to God, and to each other.

Finally, to ascend to the highest sphere of all, the Hebrews had, like other ancient nations, a national Deity, whose name was Jehovah. The national Deity of the Hebrews, unlike those of other nations, was God indeed. All His attributes were those of the true God, though but partially revealed: and His worship has consequently passed into the worship of the Universal Father without break or incongruity, as the light of dawn brightens and broadens into the light of day. But it is as God the universal Father of all that He is worshipped by Christians, not as Jehovah the Deity of the Hebrew nation.

[s] Deut. x. 12—22.

SECTION II.

Having thus seen the relation of the Old Testament to primitive institutions, customs, and ideas generally, we come to the particular case of Slavery.

Slavery is found existing in all barbarous nations, from the Chinese to the ancient Germans. Civilized nations have gradually emerged from it. Russia, the last born of civilization, has just emancipated her serfs. Within the pale of Christendom, the institution now remains only in the Slave-owning communities of America, and in the dependencies of Spain. And in these countries it is found in connection with a certain kind of agriculture, which is supposed to require negro labourers working in large gangs. In the Dutch dependency of Java it exists in a qualified form, and the party of humanity in Holland is now demanding its abolition.

The authors of the Declaration of Independence, on which the American Constitution, for the Slave as well as for the Free States, is founded, say, "We hold these truths to be self-evident; that all men are created equal; that they are endowed by their Creator with certain inalienable rights; that among these are life, liberty, and the pursuit of happiness; and that to secure these rights, governments are instituted among men, deriving their just powers from the consent of the governed." Supposing the negro to be a man, the Slave-owners who have set their hands to these sentiments have pronounced the doom of their own institution and saved its adversaries further trouble. But it must in fairness to them be owned that they have set their hands to too much. It can scarcely be held that liberty, political or personal, is the inalienable right of every human being. Children possess neither political nor personal liberty, till they arrive at what the law, a law which they had no share in making, pronounces to be years of discretion. Women have no political liberties, and married women have personal liberties only of a very qualified kind. Under despotic governments, the immorality of which can scarcely be held to be in all cases self-evident, no one has political liberty. Even under constitutional governments where the suffrage is limited, as it is to some extent in most of those which are commonly called free countries, the unenfranchised classes are as destitute of political liberty as the subjects of a despotism. The political power which commands their obedience is vested, it is true, in a greater number of hands, and is on that account more controlled by the influence of opinion, and less liable to gross abuse; but it commands their obedience as absolutely and as irrespectively of their own consent, as though it were that of a despotic Prince. The equality between man and man on which this indefeasible claim to political and personal liberty is founded, is in truth rather a metaphysical notion than a fact. Not only children and the weaker sex, but the great mass of men, are so constituted by nature, or so circumstanced, as to be inevitably dependent upon others; and to say that they have an equal right to independence with those on whom they are necessarily dependent, would be an abuse, or at least a very barren use, of words. That to which every moral being has an indefeasible right, besides life, is the "pursuit of happiness." In other words, he has a right to have his moral interests considered and respected, and not to be treated as a being having no moral interests of his own,—a mere "living tool," as the slave is called by Aristotle, or a "chattel personal," as he is called by the American law. Every moral being has a right, in other words, to be treated by the community as a person, and not as a thing. And in every state of society which is sound, however primitive it may be, and however remote from our advanced ideas of political and personal liberty, these conditions of respecting the moral interests of each member, and of treating each member as a person, not as a thing, are fulfilled. One man may be dependent upon another to any extent, in certain circumstances he may be absolutely dependent, without prejudice to the morality of the relations between them. But morality is at once violated when the interest of one man is sacrificed to that of another, and a state of things then commences noxious to the moral being of both parties, and more noxious to the moral being of him who commits, than to that of him who endures the wrong. Judge Ruffin of North Carolina, in giving judgment on the extent of the master's dominion over the slave in that country, said, "The question before the Court has indeed been assimilated at the bar to the other domestic relations; and arguments drawn from the well-established principles which confer and restrain the authority of the parent over the child, the tutor over the pupil, the master over the apprentice, have been pressed on us. The Court does not recognise their application. There is no likeness between the cases. They are in opposition to each other, and there is an impassable gulf between them. The difference is that which exists between freedom and slavery, and a greater cannot be imagined. In the one, the end in view is the happiness of the youth, born to equal rights with that governor, on whom the duty devolves of training the young to usefulness in a station which he is afterwards to assume among freemen. To such an end, and with such a subject, moral and intellectual instruction seem the natural means; and for the most part they are found to suffice. Moderate force is superadded, only to make the others effectual. If that fail, it is better to leave the party to his own headstrong passions, and the ultimate correction of the law, than to allow it to be immoderately inflicted by a private person. With slavery it is far otherwise. The end is the profit of the master, his security, and the public safety; the subject, one doomed in his own person and his posterity to live without knowledge, and without the capacity to make anything his own, and to toil that another may reap the fruits. What moral considerations shall be addressed to such a being, to convince him what it is impossible but that the most stupid must feel and know can never be true, —that he is thus to labour upon a principle of natural duty, or for the sake of his own personal happiness. Such services can only be expected from one who has no will of his own, who surrenders his will in implicit obedience to that of another."

The relation thus judicially described is an immoral relation, because it sacrifices not merely the personal or political liberties, but the moral interests of one party to the other. It is a relation, therefore, which could never exist in any state of society, however rude, which was founded on morality; nor be sanctioned under any dispensation really emanating from the Author of our moral nature. But a relation of the most complete dependence may be perfectly moral. Nothing is more moral than the relation between a mother and her infant child.

Let us observe also that the relation described by the words of Judge Ruffin is perfectly definite and distinct. It is that of a slave, not that of a servant bound for a term of years or for life, or even of a hereditary bondman who retains any personal rights and is not wholly devoted to the profit and pleasure of his master. There can be no pretence for refining it away into a 'certain condition of the labourer, accidentally denoted by a name derived from the hatred felt by other nations for the Sclavonic race.' We may be permitted to add, that this definite relation is marked by definite characteristics, in regard to the treatment of women, of fathers and of husbands, which are well known to the whole civilized world.

On approaching the question from the side of the Old Testament, we are met by an assertion which, if it be true, sweeps the field of controversy at once. It is said that we are bound to keep the negro race in bondage for ever in order to fulfil the inspired prophecy of Noah, "Cursed be Canaan; a servant of servants shall he be unto his brethren. . . . Blessed be the Lord God of Shem; and Canaan shall be his servant. God shall enlarge Japheth, and he shall dwell in the tents of Shem; and Canaan shall be his servant." So scrupulous is the reverence of the Slaveowners for Scripture, so great is their zeal for God's honour, that upon a merely conjectural interpretation of a passage in the most obscure and difficult part of the Bible, they feel bound to condemn to hopeless slavery on their plantations a whole race of mankind who, in common with the other races, have been redeemed by Christ.

To all arguments of this kind there is, in the first place, a very simple answer, which has already been given, in effect, to those who thought it their duty as Christians to fulfil inspired prophecy by denying civil rights to the Jews. Man is not charged with the fulfilment of inspired prophecy, which, whatever he may do, will certainly fulfil itself; but he is charged with the performance of his duty to his neighbour. It is not incumbent upon him to preserve Divine Foreknowledge from disappointment, but it is incumbent upon him to preserve his own soul from injustice, cruelty, and lust. If the prophecy had meant that the negroes should always be slaves, it would have been defeated already, for a great part of the negroes in Africa have never become slaves, and those in the English and French colonies, besides a good many in America itself, have ceased to be so.

In the second place, those who found slavery on a doom pronounced against the negro race must say no more about the recognition of their institution by the law of Moses or by the New Testament, for the slavery recognised by the law of Moses and the New Testament was not that of negroes, but of other races.

But the truth is, that the words of Noah, to whomsoever they may apply, are no prophecy, but only a curse, couched in the language of Oriental malediction; and all curses have been taken away by Christ. This curse was taken away even before Christ, when Abraham was told that "in his seed all the nations of the earth should be blessed."

To come, then, to that which is more to the purpose. The latest researches of historical philosophy seem to lead us back to the simplest and most natural theory of the origin of society, and to shew us that the political systems which now fill the world, with all their grandeur and complexity, once lay enfolded in the Patriarch's tent. So that in the Patriarchal chief of an Arabian tribe we still see the father of Empires and Republics [t].

While society was in the Patriarchal state, each family or tribe being independent of the rest, there was of course no general government. The only government was the family despotism, which, as we have already had occasion to observe, was prolonged among the Romans, through hatred of change and love of power, into a much later stage of civilization. The only law for every member of the family was the

[t] See Maine's Ancient Law, ch. v.

father's will, which is now merged, for all children who have come to manhood, in the law of the State. His lips pronounced the blessing and the curse, which can now be pronounced without absurdity only by the moral judgment of society at large. Such a despotism was in fact necessary to the existence of each of these primitive communities. Had it been bound together by any looser bond, it would have perished in the perpetual contest with its competitors for the hunting-ground, the pasture, and the springs of water, or have been swallowed up by the wilderness, amidst the terrors and dangers of which these little germs of social existence must have hung between life and death.

It is on this state of society, but at a late period of it, that the history of the Hebrews opens. The original family has broadened into a tribe or clan by taking into it members not of its own blood; the wreck, perhaps, of other families which had perished in the primæval struggle for existence. These new members are servants to the head of the tribe, on whose protection their lives must depend. Nations with regular governments, and distinctions of class, have been formed in the countries on the edge of which Abraham and his tribe wander. In these nations slavery exists. Its first source probably was war; a further supply being obtained, when the value of the slave to the indolent warrior was felt, by piracy and kidnapping. The traffic in men, which is the strongest evidence of the existence of Slavery in the true sense of the term, has commenced. Abraham himself, from his commerce with slave-owning nations, has servants "bought with his money," as well as servants "born in his house."

But the bondage of Abraham's servants, whether born in his house or bought with his money, can scarcely be called slavery. It is domestic, not merely in the modern, but in the patriarchal sense of the term. In the lonely encampment the head of the tribe must live entirely with his servants. He has no other companions or friends. He is not a member of a class of freemen, nor are they members of a class of slaves: no feeling of contempt therefore can arise in his mind, nor of degradation in theirs. He and his children work as they do. Jacob seethes the pottage while Esau seeks food by hunting, and the patriarch feels it no disgrace to serve Laban as a common herdsman.

The son is a bondman as well as the servant. Under the family despotism of the Romans he could obtain his liberty only by thrice going through the form of being sold by his father as a slave; and then he ceased to be, in the fullest sense, a member of the family. The eldest son alone was distinguished above the rest of those "in the father's hand," by having the birthright and being the destined head of the tribe in his turn. And if there was no son, a bondman took the inheritance. "And Abram said, Lord God, what wilt Thou give me, seeing I go childless, and the steward of my house is this Eliezer of Damascus? And Abram said, Behold, to me Thou hast given no seed: and, lo, one born in my house is mine heir[u]."

When the family rite of circumcision, the pledge of

[u] Gen. xv. 2, 3.

religious unity, is performed, all the bondmen, whether born in the house or bought with money, are circumcised. "And Abraham took Ishmael his son, and all that were born in his house, and all that were bought with his money, every male among the men of Abraham's house; and circumcised the flesh of their foreskin in the selfsame day, as God had said unto him[x]." "He that is born in thy house, and he that is bought with thy money, must needs be circumcised: and My covenant shall be in your flesh for an everlasting covenant."

Here is the picture of Patriarchal Bondage: "And Abraham was old, and well stricken in age: and the Lord had blessed Abraham in all things. And Abraham said unto his eldest servant of his house, that ruled over all that he had, Put, I pray thee, thy hand under my thigh: and I will make thee swear by the Lord, the God of heaven, and the God of the earth, that thou shalt not take a wife unto my son of the daughters of the Canaanites, among whom I dwell: but thou shalt go unto my country, and to my kindred, and take a wife unto my son Isaac. . . . . And the servant took ten camels of the camels of his master, and departed; for all the goods of his master were in his hand: and he arose, and went to Mesopotamia, unto the city of Nahor. And he made his camels to kneel down without the city by a well of water at the time of the evening, even the time that women go out to draw water. And he said, O Lord God of my master Abraham, I pray Thee, send me good speed this day,

[x] Gen. xvii. 23.

and shew kindness unto my master Abraham. Behold, I stand here by the well of water; and the daughters of the men of the city come out to draw water: and let it come to pass, that the damsel to whom I shall say, Let down thy pitcher, I pray thee, that I may drink; and she shall say, Drink, and I will give thy camels drink also: let the same be she that Thou hast appointed for Thy servant Isaac; and thereby shall I know that Thou hast shewed kindness unto my master ^y."

In the picture, on which the evening sun of a long-vanished world here falls, we see, it may safely be said, a relation widely different from that which is painted in the decision of Judge Ruffin. It is a relation of perfect affection and confidence, of complete identity of interest, between the master and the servant. If the analogies of tutor and pupil, master and apprentice, which Judge Ruffin rejects in the case of American Slavery, are not applicable in this case, it is only because the strongest of them is too weak: and assuredly the term "chattel personal" applied to the steward as he stands by the well praying God to be good to his master, would grate strangely on our ears.

This passage illustrates not only the position of the bondman in the family, but the relative position of the son. We see that in the matter of marriage, he was entirely "in his father's hand." So in the Roman family, the father could marry any one of his children or of their children, and divorce them, at his pleasure.

^y Gen. xxiv. 1—4, 10—14.

That the father, in the patriarchal state, as well as at Rome, had the power of life and death over the son, as much as he could have it over the bondman, we see from the story in which Abraham consents to sacrifice Isaac, without any scruple on the ground of moral right, though doubtless with the deepest feelings of paternal sorrow. Ignorance of this fact has led to mistaken judgments, sometimes expressed in very strong language, as to the morality of the story, which, in its issue, is an abrogation of human sacrifices, such as were offered by the neighbouring nations, who made their children pass through the fire to Moloch.

It will also be seen from the same passage that the oath of a bondman was as good as that of a freeman. "Put, I pray thee, thy hand under my thigh: and I will make thee swear by the Lord, the God of heaven, and the God of the earth," &c. In Greece during the classical times, or at Rome, a bondman's oath would have been worth little. It would scarcely have been supposed that the Gods stooped to guard the faith or punish the perjury of a Slave.

The servant prays to God and blesses Him as "the God of his master Abraham" because the persons of all the tribe were gathered up as it were into the sacred person of the chief, and came into relation with God and with other tribes through him. So at Rome, the father of the family represented all its members before the Gods and the State.

Laban, the free head of a family, receives Abraham's servant quite as an equal. "And he said, Come in, thou blessed of the Lord; wherefore standest thou without? for I have prepared the house, and room for the camels." And on the other hand, Jacob, though he has the birthright, and is to be head of his tribe, binds himself to serve Laban for twice seven years, not exactly as a bondman, but doing the same kind of work as the bondmen did, and surrendering his personal liberty to his master in a way which would not now be permitted (except in the peculiar case of military service) by the laws of any country in which civilized morality prevails.

The identity of interest between the Patriarchal chief and his servant, and the reliance consequently placed by the chief in the servant's loyalty, which we have noted in the story of Abraham's steward, appear elsewhere also. "When Abraham heard that his brother (Lot) was taken captive, he armed his trained servants, born in his own house, three hundred and eighteen, and pursued them unto Dan." The herdmen of Abraham and Lot (Gen. xiii.) and the herdmen of Isaac and Gerar (Gen. xxvi.) strive of their own accord for the pastures and the wells of springing water, evidently regarding the interest of their master as their own.

So much respecting the nature of bondage in the patriarchal state. It seems to bear little resemblance to the condition of the gangs of negro chattels who are driven out under the lash of an overseer to plant cotton in America, and who are slaves to the tyrannical cruelty and lust of the white members of their owner's family, as well as to the avarice of their owner. When we find a negro standing in the same relation to his master, and to his master's son, in which Eliezer stood to Abraham and Isaac, and when we find in negro slavery the other characteristics of bondage as it existed in the tents of Abraham and his descendants, we may begin to think that the term "Patriarchal" is true as applied to the Slavery of Virginia and Carolina.

SECTION III.

WHEN we come to the time of Moses and his laws, we find society at a more advanced stage. The families have become united in the tribe; and the tribes are fast blending into the nation. All the features of national life will now appear. Classes will be formed, and the difference between the freeman and the bondman will be distinctly felt. The State, though in a rude shape, will take the place of the head of the family as the ruler and protector of all: so that the protection afforded by his master will no longer make up to the bondman for the loss of personal liberty. The time is fast approaching when bondage will become an evil and a wrong.

Still, that time has not yet quite arrived. Society is not yet so settled, nor law so paramount, but that protection may be sometimes better for the poor man than independence. The history of the Book of Judges is filled with violence: and the passages of the Law which speak of the hired labourer and assert his rights shew that his condition, before public opinion had begun to guard the poor, was hard, and liable to oppression. Achilles in Homer, when he wishes to express the dreariness of the realms below, says that he would rather be the hired labourer of a poor man than reign over all the Dead.

Accordingly we find that servitude among the Hebrews is sometimes voluntary. "And it shall be, if he (the bondman) say unto thee, I will not go away from thee; because he loveth thee and thine house, because he is well with thee; then thou shalt take an awl and thrust it through his ear into the door, and he shall be thy servant for ever. And also unto thy maidservant thou shalt do likewise[z]." So in the early part of the Middle Ages, amidst the wild unsettlement of the times, many persons gave up their independence for the protection of a lord.

Slavery was domestic among the Hebrews, as it is generally in the East. The slave would live constantly with his master, have daily opportunities of winning his regard, and derive from his society all the benefits which an inferior can derive from the society of a superior. On the great American plantations, on the contrary, the slaves live in "quarters" of their own, separate from the whites: they work in the field by themselves all day, no white being present but the overseer. The master of the plantation seldom appears upon the scene of labour, and barely knows his human chattels by sight. In fact, the overseer is often the only white with whom the slaves come into con-

[z] Deut. xv. 16, 17.

tact the whole year round, and even he only just knows enough of them to call them by name[a]. So that there cannot possibly be any kind relations between master and slave, nor any mental training and elevation of the slave by intercourse with his master, such as the defenders of slavery would have us suppose to exist, and such as really existed under the Patriarchs and among the Hebrews in the time of Moses. If we want a parallel to the relations of master and slave on the American plantations, we must seek it not among the people of Jehovah, but in the gangs of Athenian slaves who worked the mines of Laurium, or in the "field-hands" who tilled the great estates of Roman nobles, and who dwelt like the negroes in slave quarters and worked in droves under the lash. The Roman writers on agriculture indeed might afford manuals for the American planters. Cato, who was a perfect model of the slave-owning agriculturist, advises his reader to "sell off his old oxen, his discarded cows and sheep, wool, hides, old wagons, old tools, *old and sickly slaves.*"

The sentiments of the master and bondman, and their education, in the age and country for which Moses made laws, would be much the same. No high-bred contempt therefore would be felt by the master for the slave: there would be none of the pride which breathes through the language held by the American slave-owners as to the expediency of dooming the lower class to slavery that the upper class may have leisure for higher cultivation. Nor had the slightest taint of degradation yet attached to labour, which was

[a] Olmsted, Journey in the Back Country, p. 72.

still the equal lot of all. The seven daughters of Jethro, the priest of Midian, "came and drew water, and filled the troughs to water their father's flock[b]." Moses keeps the sheep of his father-in-law. The wealthy Boaz mingles with his reapers in a way in which no great planter would mingle with his slave-gang, and he lies down himself on the threshing-floor to guard the corn at night. In this respect the feelings of men had not changed since that earlier age when Jacob was Laban's shepherd.

In politics, too, we are far from those aristocratic liberties of republics which make slavery bitter indeed. In the time of Moses, the thought of political liberty has perhaps scarcely awakened in any breast. In the time of the Monarchy all are alike servants of the king.

Long after this the relation between master and servant might serve a sacred poet as the type of a relation which, though that of the most complete dependence, is the most beneficent as well as the holiest of all. "Behold, even as the eyes of servants look unto the hand of their masters, and as the eyes of a maiden unto the hand of her mistress: even so our eyes wait upon the Lord our God until He have mercy upon us[c]."

In fact, the state of things among the Hebrews in the time of Moses very much resembles that which the poems of Homer disclose to us as existing in heroic Greece; where society is still in course of transition from the family to the nation; where slavery is domestic and on the whole mild, the lot of the slave under

---

[b] Exod. ii. 16.   [c] Ps. cxxiii. 2.

an average master being probably not worse than that of the hired labourer [d]; where Paris, a king's son, keeps his flock on Ida, and Nausicaa, a king's daughter, goes out with her handmaidens to wash linen at the spring; where the faithful swineherd Eumæus stands almost upon a level with freemen, is treated by Ulysses as a friend, and is deeply attached to his master and his master's house; but where, nevertheless, "A man loses half his manhood on the day when he becomes a slave."

Such is the slavery with which the Hebrew Lawgiver deals: and he deals with it, as it was before said that he deals with rude institutions generally, not to establish or perpetuate it, but to mitigate it, restrict it, and prepare the way for its abolition. That he did not introduce it we know; since we see it existing before him in the Patriarchal age.

To keep a Hebrew in perpetual bondage, except by his own consent, is absolutely forbidden. "If thou buy an Hebrew servant, six years he shall serve; and in the seventh he shall go out free for nothing [e]." "If thy brother, an Hebrew man, or an Hebrew woman, be sold unto thee, and serve thee six years; then in the seventh year thou shalt let him go free from thee [f]." "It shall not seem hard unto thee, when thou sendest him away free from thee; for he hath been worth a double hired servant to thee, in serving thee six years: and the Lord thy God shall bless thee in all that thou doest." The occurrence of the year of jubilee might cut the term of servitude still shorter [g]. And even

[d] Grote, vol. ii. p. 133.
[e] Exod. xxi. 2.
[f] Deut. xv. 12.
[g] Levit. xxv. 41.

while that term lasted the servant was not to be treated as a slave, a "living tool" or a "chattel personal." "If thy brother that dwelleth by thee be waxen poor, and be sold unto thee; thou shalt not compel him to serve as a bondservant: but as an hired servant, and as a sojourner, he shall be with thee, and shall serve thee unto the year of jubilee: and then shall he depart from thee, both he and his children with him, and shall return unto his own family, and unto the possession of his fathers shall he return. For they are my servants, which I brought forth out of the land of Egypt: they shall not be sold as bondmen. Thou shalt not rule over him with rigour; but shalt fear thy God[h]."

The bondman might choose, as we have seen, at the expiration of his term to remain with his master instead of accepting his liberty; but to that end, and in order that a freeman might be finally divested of his freedom, not a mere tacit continuance of the relation, but a formal consent, and not only a formal consent, but a regular and public ceremony, was required. The bondman is to "say plainly" that he "loves his master," and that he "will not go out free." And he is then to be brought before the judges, and his ear is to be bored with an awl, as a sign that he elects to remain in servitude for life.

That the bondman when set free after six years might not fall into bondage again, he was to be liberally provided on leaving his master with the means of subsistence. "And when thou sendest him out free from thee, thou shalt not let him go away empty: thou shalt

[h] Levit. xxv. 39—43.

furnish him liberally out of thy flock, and out of thy floor, and out of thy winepress: of that wherewith the Lord thy God hath blessed thee, thou shalt give unto him. And thou shalt remember that thou wast a bondman in the land of Egypt, and the Lord thy God redeemed thee: therefore I command thee this thing to-day[i]."

Moreover, the Hebrew who had been driven by poverty to sell himself to a stranger or a sojourner, might be redeemed at any time either by himself, or by his kinsman, on payment of the fair value of his service for the term yet remaining[j].

A housebreaker, not punished in the fact, and unable to make full restitution, is to be sold for his theft; and it appears, into slavery for life[k]. But this being a case of penal bondage, does not bear upon the present question. It is the counterpart not of modern slavery, but of modern transportation.

Thus, so long as the law of Moses was kept, the bondage of a Hebrew would not be more severe, either in duration or in other respects, than a modern apprenticeship, nor so severe as the forced service of a soldier in a modern army: and he would receive what would be equivalent to wages in the shape of a gift at parting when his term expired. Such servitude was in fact not slavery at all, in the proper sense of the term.

The law of Moses was not always kept in this any more than in other respects; but it was not a dead letter. "This is the word that came unto Jeremiah

[i] Deut. xv. 13—15.   [j] Levit. xxv. 47.   [k] Exod. xxii. 3.

from the Lord, after that the king Zedekiah had made a covenant with all the people which were at Jerusalem, to proclaim liberty unto them; that every man should let his manservant, and every man his maidservant, being an Hebrew or an Hebrewess, go free; that none should serve himself of them, to wit, of a Jew his brother. Now when all the princes, and all the people, which had entered into the covenant, heard that every one should let his manservant, and every one his maidservant, go free, that none should serve themselves of them any more, then they obeyed, and let them go. But afterward they turned, and caused the servants and the handmaids, whom they had let go free, to return, and brought them into subjection for servants and for handmaids. Therefore the word of the Lord came to Jeremiah from the Lord, saying, Thus saith the Lord, the God of Israel; I made a covenant with your fathers in the day that I brought them forth out of the land of Egypt, out of the house of bondmen, saying, At the end of seven years let ye go every man his brother an Hebrew, which hath been sold unto thee; and when he hath served thee six years, thou shalt let him go free from thee: but your fathers hearkened not unto Me; neither inclined their ear. And ye were now turned, and had done right in My sight, in proclaiming liberty every man to his neighbour; and ye had made a covenant before Me in the house which is called by My name: but ye turned and polluted My name, and caused every man his servant, and every man his handmaid, whom he had set at liberty at their pleasure, to return, and brought them into subjection, to be unto you for servants and for handmaids. Therefore thus saith the Lord; Ye have not hearkened unto Me, in proclaiming liberty, every one to his brother, and every man to his neighbour: behold, I proclaim a liberty for you, saith the Lord, to the sword, to the pestilence, and to the famine; and I will make you to be removed into all the kingdoms of the earth[1]."

Neither the Greek nor the Roman had any scruple in reducing one of his own countrymen to that permanent bondage which alone can be properly called slavery. In the early times both of Athens and Rome, we find numbers of the poor reduced to slavery by the rich. And in the wars between Grecian states, whole communities when vanquished are swept into hopeless and irredeemable bondage by the people of their own race. Greece must have swarmed with Greek slaves after the Peloponnesian war.

Foreign slaves the Hebrew was permitted to hold. "Both thy bondmen, and thy bondmaids, which thou shalt have, shall be of the heathen that are round about you; of them shall ye buy bondmen and bondmaids. Moreover of the children of the strangers that do sojourn among you, of them shall ye buy, and of their families that are with you, which they begat in your land: and they shall be your possession. And ye shall take them as an inheritance for your children after you, to inherit them for a possession; they shall be your bondmen for ever: but over your brethren the children of Israel, ye shall not rule one over an-

[1] Jer. xxxiv. 8—17.

other with rigour [m]." These words are the continuation of those before quoted from Leviticus respecting the liberation of Hebrew bondmen, and must be construed in connection with them. The object of the whole passage is to forbid the holding of Hebrew, not to command or encourage the holding of foreign, slaves. We shall presently see whether the Mosaic institutions tended practically to the multiplication of slaves of any kind.

Fortunate, probably, in a world of bondage, was the bondman who served in a Hebrew household and under the Hebrew law; nor would he have been morally the gainer by being sent back from the kingdom of Jehovah into that of Moloch, Baal, Rimmon, or Astarte. The Lawgiver knew the abominations of the heathen, and we shall see that he was not without regard for the religious interests of the foreign slave.

It must be remembered also that in war, as carried on in ancient times, the lot of the vanquished was slavery, or death. To have prohibited slavery then, as regards foreign captives, would have been in effect to enact that every prisoner, of whatever age or sex, taken in war, should be put to death.

The reason, however, why a Hebrew was allowed to hold a foreigner while he was not allowed to hold another Hebrew as a slave, is clear from the words of the law; and it is equally clear that it is one which has long since passed away. The Hebrew *was his brother*, the foreigner *was not his brother*. But under

[m] Levit. xxv. 44—46.

the Christian dispensation all men are brethren in Christ.

It would be the reverse of the truth to say, with the Roman satirist, that the Hebrews, compared with the other nations of antiquity, were exclusive and inhospitable towards foreigners and people of other religions: that they " would not direct on his road the man who did not worship as they did, nor guide to the spring any but the circumcised." Their law, on the contrary, breathes a spirit of kindness and hospitality towards the stranger quite unexampled in that hard and inhospitable world. The Greek, though his mind was large and his intercourse varied, called all nations but his own by a name of opprobrium and contempt; and his treatment of them was quite in accordance with that name, till one of them conquered him, when his former pride towards all sank into sycophancy towards the conqueror. The humane Athenians, in the time of Pericles, Phidias, and Sophocles, revised the list of citizens, and having discovered that five thousand persons not of pure Athenian blood had crept into the register, not only expelled them, but sold them all as slaves. The Roman had one word for foreigner and enemy, nor was his language belied by his conduct towards his neighbours. The Hebrew is repeatedly and most emphatically enjoined by his law to be kind to the stranger and never to oppress him; and this on the ground, so humbling to national pride, that he had been himself an oppressed and despised dweller in a strange land. " Thou shalt neither vex a stranger, nor oppress him : for ye were strangers in the land of

Egypt[n]." "Also thou shalt not oppress a stranger: for ye know the heart of a stranger, seeing ye were strangers in the land of Egypt[o]." And in a still more solemn passage: "For the Lord your God is God of gods, and Lord of lords, a great God, a mighty, and a terrible, which regardeth not persons, nor taketh reward: He doth execute the judgment of the fatherless and widow, and loveth the stranger, in giving him food and raiment. Love ye therefore the stranger: for ye were strangers in the land of Egypt[p]." "Ye shall have one manner of law, as well for the stranger, as for one of your own country: for I am the Lord your God[q]." But nevertheless the Hebrew did not understand, nor, without a miracle which would have made the shadow go down two thousand years on the sundial of history, could he have understood the brotherhood of man; much less that higher brotherhood by which all men are united in Christ.

When the scene of history opens, the nations are simply competitors for existence, bound together by no laws or sympathies, but preying on each other like the wild beasts of the forest, and having each its own national God, who is an enemy to the Gods of the other nations. Devotion to his nation was the most comprehensive, and therefore the highest, bond of affection which man then knew; and his moral eye could see nothing but patriotic virtue in the deeds of Scævola and Ehud, or in the triumphal song of Deborah over the fall (it mattered not by what means) of the grand

[n] Exod. xxii. 21.
[o] Ibid. xxiii. 9.
[p] Deut. x. 17—19.
[q] Levit. xxiv. 22.

enemy and oppressor of Israel. And this patriotism, narrow as it seems to our enlarged perceptions, was a step in the training of humanity midway between devotion to the tribe and devotion to the kind. The rivulet found its river; perhaps, at some far distant day, the river may find its sea; and as the tribe was merged in the nation, the nation may be merged in the community of man. Already the sharp outline of national distinction begins to be blurred by religious, intellectual, and commercial union. The time may come when our views may seem as narrow and our conduct as selfish to posterity, as the views of antiquity seem narrow and its conduct selfish to us. However that may be, whether the movement which has been going on since the beginning of history has now found its term or not, gradual progress, in which human effort should play its part, not miraculous anticipation of the future, was, as we have before said, the rule of Providence in dealing with the Hebrews as well as with other races. And a Hebrew broke no law of affection known to him, he did no violence to his moral nature, no injury to any one who to him was a brother, by holding a man of another nation as a slave.

An American even if he had lived in the time of Moses, and under the Mosaic law, would not have been allowed by the spirit of that law to sell or hold as a slave a man or woman as white and essentially of the same race as himself, much less his own child. But the Americans do not live in the time of Moses, nor under the Mosaic law. They live in times when the brotherhood of man is known, and the duty of treating all men as brethren is understood; they live under, and will be judged by, the law of Christ.

There is indeed one passage (Exod. xxi. 7) which is cited by American defenders of slavery as divinely authorizing a Christian to sell his own child as a slave: "And if a man sell his daughter to be a maidservant, she shall not go out as the menservants do." But read on, and it will appear that the passage has nothing to do with this matter. "If she please not her master, who hath betrothed her to himself, then shall he let her be redeemed: to sell her unto a strange nation he shall have no power, seeing he hath dealt deceitfully with her. And if he have betrothed her unto his son, he shall deal with her after the manner of daughters. If he take him another wife; her food, her raiment, and her duty of marriage, shall he not diminish. And if he do not these three unto her, then shall she go out free without money." Clearly this refers to the sale and purchase of a woman, not as a slave, but as a wife; though a wife of an inferior kind, such as the concubine of the Levite in the Book of Judges who has fled from her lord, and whom he pursues to her father's house. Such a mode of providing for a daughter and obtaining a wife was familiar enough to the coarseness of primitive antiquity, not only in the Jewish but in other nations. The Anglo-Saxons in the earliest times regularly sold their daughters as wives, and their laws speak of buying women in the plainest terms. The recognition of the practice in the Mosaic law is important to the present question, as shewing us that it is with the earliest and rudest state of society that we are dealing. But it in no way authorizes a Christian to sell his daughter as a slave.

Among the Romans the master had absolute power of life and death over the slave. Still more had he the power of punishing him to any extent, and doing him any bodily injury he pleased. It was not till the time of Seneca, when influences closely connected with Christianity, if not Christianity itself, had begun to work on Roman Jurisprudence, that the power of the master was in any way limited, or that the person of the slave received any protection from the law. Vedius Pollio, a wealthy Roman, and a friend of Augustus, used, when his slaves displeased him, to throw them alive into his fishpond to feed his lampreys. One day a slave who had broken a crystal goblet, flung himself at the feet of the Emperor, who was supping with Pollio, praying, not that his life might be spared, but that he might not be given as food to the fishes. Augustus rebuked, but did not punish or even discard, his friend[r]. "If," says Horace, "a man is thought mad who crucifies his slave for having filched something from a dish which he has taken off the table, how much more mad must he be who cuts his friend for a trifling offence[s]." The Roman lady in Juvenal orders a cross to be set up for a slave, and when her husband asks the reason of the punishment, and desires her to pause before she takes away a man's life, she ridicules the notion that a slave is a man, and says that her will is reason enough.

[r] Dion Cassius, liv. 23 ; Senec. De Ira, iii. 40; De Clem. xviii.
[s] Hor. Sat., I. iii. 80.

The Hebrew Lawgiver does not set aside the general constitution of the family, and the general prerogatives of its head. He could not have done so without tearing up the very foundations of society in that age. But he places the life and limb of the slave for the first time under the protection of the law. "And if a man smite his servant, or his maid, with a rod, and he die under his hand; he shall be surely punished. Notwithstanding, if he continue a day or two, he shall not be punished: for he is his money[t]." "And if a man smite the eye of his servant, or the eye of his maid, that it perish; he shall let him go free for his eye's sake. And if he smite out his manservant's tooth, or his maidservant's tooth; he shall let him go free for his tooth's sake[u]."

This, no doubt, is one of the things given to the Jews because of the hardness of their hearts; because they had not as yet attained, nor could they as yet have attained, the high social morality of modern and Christian times. The protection afforded by this law to the person of the slave is small in itself; but it is a great step in humanity compared with his totally unprotected condition among the Romans, far more advanced in general civilization as they were, and even with the protection afforded him among the Anglo-Saxons, not only in their heathen state, but after their conversion to Christianity. "In the earliest period," says a writer on Anglo-Saxon institutions, "the master had the power of life and death over the slave, and with it all the inferior rights which flow from it.

[t] Exod. xxi. 20.   [u] Ibid. xxi. 26, 27.

In the exercise of this terrible power, both the early continental Germans and their Anglo-Saxon descendants abstained from acts of deliberate cruelty. It was not usual with the Germans to punish their slaves with whips or chains, or to oppress them with uncertain exactions. No law, however, protected their lives; and though they were never put to death deliberately, they were often slain in fits of passion. The earliest laws of the Anglo-Saxons were in accordance with Germanic customs. They *permitted* the master to put his slave to death when, where, and how he pleased; and the first modification of this barbarous right, which emanated from the clergy, was so slight, that it could have but little influence on national manners[x]." Even the intentional beating to death of a slave was punished only by penitential fasting, the rigour of which Anglo-Saxon casuistry found means effectually to evade. And for the knocking out an eye or tooth the Church *advised* the master to give the slave his freedom, but the law did not compel it.

The expression "he shall be surely punished" in the Hebrew law just cited, is indefinite; and Michaelis thinks that it cannot be taken as meaning capital punishment, though no fine or other secondary punishment is specified. But it must be observed that the law speaks not of wilful murder, but of excessive chastisement inflicted by the "rod" of the master and unintentionally resulting in death. There seems to be nothing to take the wilful murder of a bondman, whether by his master or by any other person, out of

[x] Thrupp's Anglo-Saxon Home, p. 126.

the general sentence "Whosoever sheddeth man's blood by man shall his blood be shed." This sentence is repeatedly and emphatically ratified by the Mosaic Law, "He that smiteth a man so that he die, he shall surely be put to death." "He that killeth any man shall surely be put to death." It is expressly enacted that the punishment of death shall be inflicted on the murderer of an alien as well as on the murderer of a Hebrew[y]. It is not likely that more protection would be given to the life of the alien than to that of the Hebrew bondman, who is treated throughout as a member of the commonwealth, though his labour for a certain time belongs to another. And the law draws no distinction in these respects between the Hebrew bondman and the foreign slave.

By parity of reasoning both classes of bondmen would seem to be protected, as against any one but their master, by the general law respecting personal injuries. "And if a man cause a blemish in his neighbour; as he hath done, so shall it be done to him; breach for breach, eye for eye, tooth for tooth: as he hath caused a blemish in a man, so shall it be done to him again[z]."

To the Hebrew slave the fact that he was his master's money would always be a real, though not always a sufficient protection. The interest of the master would never lead him to use his slaves up, as it appears slaves are sometimes used up by capitalists on the great Cuban plantations. To this kind of slow murder, against which it would be scarcely possible for any

[y] Levit. xxiv. 22.   [z] Ibid. xxiv. 19, 20.

slave law to guard, 'Hebrew agriculture could offer no temptations.

Plato in his Laws prescribes that if a slave kills a freeman he shall be given up to the kinsmen of the slain man, who are not permitted on any account to spare his life, but are to be allowed to put him to death in any way they please. If a man kills the slave of another, the philosopher would have him pay double the slave's price to the master; but if he kills his own slave he is only required to go through the ceremony of purification, in order that the land may not be defiled with blood[a]. But the law of Moses says, "Ye shall not pollute the land wherein ye are: for blood it defileth the land; and the land cannot be cleansed of the blood that is shed therein, but by the blood of him that shed it." If we look at the Mosaic dispensation in itself we may regard it as peculiarly ceremonial, but if we compare it with any other dispensation except the Christian we shall probably find that instead of being peculiarly ceremonial, it is peculiarly moral.

And moreover, it is to be remembered that if the servant or slave was the "money" of his master, so, as we have seen, in some cases, was the wife; and that if the head of the family had a power which civilized morality would not endure over his servants, he had also, as we have likewise seen, a power which civilized morality would not endure over his child. In the Roman family all these prerogatives of the household despot hung together. American writers on the "Phi-

[a] Laws, bk. ix. p. 868.

losophy of Slavery," drawing their philosophy from the domestic system of the Romans, borrow the principles of barbarism and heathenism as regards the position of the servant, but they forget to extend those principles to the position of the wife and son.

The last of the Ten Commandments which we continue to use instead of the Two, shews us what was the general state of the society for which the code was framed, and fixes the real position of the slave in the household. "Thou shalt not covet thy neighbour's *house*, thou shalt not covet thy neighbour's *wife*, nor his *manservant*, nor his *maidservant*, nor his *ox*, nor his *ass*, nor anything *that is thy neighbour's.*" We see that the wife is as completely a subject of property and a part of a man's estate as a *manservant* or a *maidservant*. And when this is seen, all thought of degradation as attaching to the condition of the slave is at an end. His lot under a bad lord might be hard, and so under a bad lord might be the lot of the wife. "The institution of slavery," says one of its eulogists, "operates by contrast and comparison." It is most true: and there would be no contrast or comparison when a man's bondservant stood on the same footing as the heir of his house or the wife of his bosom.

In the Southern States of America the murder of a slave, which was formerly punishable by a fine only, is now by law a capital offence. With regard to personal injuries, the laws of the different States vary. But it seems that both with regard to murder and with regard to personal injuries the laws are practically void. Slaves are murdered, but nobody is hanged.

Slaves are brutally beaten and tortured, yet no punishment is inflicted[b].

Indeed, in most cases, it would be impossible to convict the criminal, since the evidence of a slave is not received against a freeman, and slaves must commonly be the only witnesses of murders or outrages committed by planters or overseers. Severe laws may be safely passed where the only available evidence is to be rejected. In Greece and at Rome the slave lay under the same incapacity of appearing as a witness, saving that his evidence might be taken under torture, and was then regarded by the learned in the law as forming a useful supplement to the evidence given upon oath by the freeman. "You know, gentlemen," says a Greek advocate to an Athenian court, "that the strongest evidence is produced when there are a number of witnesses both slave and free; and when the freeman can be compelled to speak by the administration of an oath, for which a freeman cares most, and slaves by pressure of a different kind, which, even though they may die under it, forces them to speak the truth[c]." And an Attic comedian recites, with ghastly pleasantry, the different modes in which the torture was applied to the slave witness by the most civilized of mankind[d]. But the law of Moses, when it fixes the number of witnesses requisite to convict a murderer, draws no distinction between the evidence of a freeman and that of a slave[e].

[b] Goodell's American Slave Code, chap. xiii., xiv.
[c] Antiphon, Περὶ τοῦ Χορευτοῦ, p. 144.
[d] Aristoph., Ran., 618.   [e] Numb. xxxv. 30; Deut. xvii. 6.

If an ox gores a manservant or a maidservant, the owner of the ox is to pay thirty shekels of silver to the owner of the servant: but besides this, the ox is to be stoned. The value of the latter enactment is that it asserts the sanctity of the servant's life: the ox is to be put out of the way as an accursed thing because it has shed the blood of man. Too much stress can scarcely be laid on this when we consider that the Hebrew lawgiver is dealing with a barbarous nation, and introducing into their rude hearts the first principles of civilization.

"I do not think," says Mr. Olmsted, "that I have ever seen the sudden death of a negro noticed in a Southern newspaper, or heard it referred to in conversation, that the loss of property, rather than the extinction of life, was not the evident occasion of interest'."

We have no trace in the criminal law of Moses or in Hebrew history of the infliction upon the slave of any cruel or servile kind of punishment from which freemen were exempt, such as the punishment of crucifixion among the Romans, or such as the punishment of burning alive, which has been sometimes inflicted on slaves, and but for the indignant protests of civilized humanity, might perhaps be still more often inflicted on them, in the Southern States. The Hebrew

---

[f] A Journey in the Back Country, p. 63. Mr. Olmsted quotes some paragraphs, one of which (from *The Rogersville Times*,) is, "Mr. Tilghman Cobb's barn at Bedford, Va., was set fire to by lightning on Friday, the 11th, and consumed. Two negroes and three horses perished in the flames."

freeman is punished with stripes for secondary offences as well as the slave.

At Rome, the slave being a mere "chattel personal," could have none of the rights of a husband or a father: he could not contract a legal marriage, nor did the woman who bore him children, or the children she bore, stand in any relation whatever to him in the eye of the law. The same was the case, we may venture to say, in all other heathen nations where slavery prevailed. It is the case also, as is too well known, in the Slave States of America, where in law a slave's marriage is a nullity, and where, in practice, husbands are sold away from their wives, children from their parents: where the human cattle are bred like sheep or swine for the market: where, in short, the whole system is a standing defiance of nature and humanity, such as it is strange to see defended or excused, under whatever stress of political passion, by English men, and still more strange to see defended or excused by English women. But the law of Moses treats the bondman in this respect also as a person, not a thing, though his labour is the property of his master, and vindicates for him the rights of a husband and a father. "If he (the servant who is let go free in the seventh year) came in by himself, he shall go out by himself: if he were married, then his wife shall go out with him. If his master have given him a wife, and she have borne him sons or daughters; the wife and her children shall be her master's, and he shall go out by himself [g]." The

[g] Exodus xxi. 3, 4.

servant's love for his wife and children is mentioned as one of the reasons why he may choose to remain in his servitude when the six years have expired. Thus the husband would never be forcibly separated from his wife and children, though in case he had received a wife from his master (which he would do with his eyes open to the legal consequences) he might have to remain in bondage in order to retain her. The amount of personal right given to the slave by this and the other provisions in his favour is probably as large as would consist with the radical constitution of society in those times: but, as has been said before, the amount of right given was not so important as the principle of giving the slave personal rights at all, which in effect makes him no longer a slave.

The existence of legalized polygamy would tend to save female slaves from becoming the victims of lawless lust, as they were in the Slave States of heathen antiquity, and as they are in the Slave States of America. The general favour shewn by the Mosaic law to purity would tend in the same direction. And so, still more, would the equal distribution of property which it encourages, and which could not fail to bring with it a general simplicity of life, and a freedom from the luxury of which slaves were the wretched ministers in the later age of Rome.

It has also been truly said that such laws as that against muzzling the ox that treads out the corn, and against seething a kid in its mother's milk, which were intended to soften the heart of the people, and dispose them to a kind treatment even of the animals in their power, would tend with still greater force to make them humane in their dealings with the slave.

It appears also from Levit. xxv. 49 that the slave might legally acquire property, since it is there said that "if he be able he may redeem himself."

If the book of Job may be taken as in any measure an index of Hebrew sentiment, the laws of the Hebrew Commonwealth were not without effect in training its members to look on the bondman not as a thing, but as a person possessing rights, and having claims to justice. "If I did despise the cause of my manservant or of my maidservant when they contended with me; what then shall I do when God riseth up? and when He visiteth, what shall I answer Him? Did not He that made me in the womb make him? And did not One fashion us in the womb[h]?"

An eminent writer speaking of Roman slavery observes, that "in earlier times religious considerations had exercised an alleviating influence, and had released the slave and the plough-ox from labour on the days enjoined for festivals and for rest." "Nothing," he goes on to say, "is more characteristic of the spirit of Cato and those who shared his sentiments than the way in which they inculcated the observance of the holyday in the letter, and evaded it in reality, by advising that while the plough should certainly be allowed to rest on these days, the slaves should even then be incessantly occupied with other labours not expressly prohibited[i]."

Perfect rest from labour on every seventh day was se-

[h] Job xxxi. 13—15. Eng. Trans.   [i] Mommsen's Rome, vol. ii. p. 368,

cured to the Hebrew bondman, not by any ordinary law, but by one of the Ten which, delivered amidst the thunders of Sinai, formed the religious and moral groundwork of the nation.

This law alleviated the lot of the feudal serf as well as that of the Hebrew bondservant. We know that by the Hebrews it was observed even with an exaggerated strictness. The observance of Sunday is legally enjoined in the Southern States, and it appears that the injunction is generally obeyed. But in Louisiana, as at Rome, property seems to have found a way in some measure to resume its rights. "There is a law of the State," said a gentleman of Louisiana to Mr. Olmsted, "that negroes shall not be worked on Sundays; but I have seen negroes at work almost every Sunday, when I have been in the country, since I have lived in Louisiana. I spent a Sunday once with a gentleman who did not work his hands at all on Sunday, even in the grinding season; and had got some of his neighbours to help him build a schoolhouse, which was used as a church on Sunday. He said there was not a plantation on either side of him, as far as he could see, where the slaves were not generally worked on Sunday; but that after the church was started several of them quitted the practice and made their negroes go to the meeting. This made others discontented; and after a year or two the planters voted new trustees to the school, and these forbade the house to be used for any other than school purposes. This was done, he had no doubt, for the purpose of breaking up the meetings, and to lessen the discontent of the slaves which were worked on Sunday[k]." Mr. Olmsted adds in a note that he also saw slaves at work every Sunday that he was in Louisiana. "The law permits slaves to be worked, I believe, on Sunday; but requires that some compensation shall be made to them when they are, such as a subsequent holyday." And who is to fix or enforce the compensation? It is scarcely possible that the same protection should be given to the slave's day of rest in a modern community, as in a community ruled by the strict and inexorable Hebrew Law.

The most important point of all remains to be mentioned. In Greece and at Rome the slave took no part in the public worship of the State. At some of the holier rites, his presence would have been a pollution[l]. If he was employed in the temples it was for menial service. We may be sure that never except as a menial did he stand near the Consul sacrificing to Latian Jupiter on the Alban Mount. He can never have been present at the dramatic festivals of Dionysus, which, under the form of a religious ceremony, were the highest school of mental culture for the Athenian people: nor can he have mounted the Acropolis in the sacred procession on the day holy to Athene[m]. He was

[k] Journeys and Explorations, vol. ii. p. 47.

[l] See on this subject M. Wallon's *Histoire de l'Esclavage dans l'Antiquité*, a work which gives the fullest account of Slavery in ancient Greece and Rome, and to which the author of this Essay has to acknowledge his obligations.

[m] Even aliens were condemned to menial services (Hydriaphoria, Skiadephoria, Scaphephoria,) at the Panathenæa. There is in Demosth. in Mid. (c. 15) a response of the Dodonean oracle to the Athenians commanding that on a certain day all the people, slaves as well as free-

F

not without a Deity indeed, for Mercury was supposed
to protect his thefts. He was permitted and encouraged
to offer gifts to his master's household Gods, and to
pray to them for blessings on his master's store, in
which he had the same sort of interest as the ox. The
festival of Saturn, the God of the primitive and conquered races from whom many of his class had sprung,
brought him a season of chartered equality and license
—an equality which only mocked his hopeless degradation; a license which was the seal of his bondage, since
it proved that his master's power was secure. That
despotism, whether social or political, must be strong,
which can afford to allow its slaves a Saturnalia.

It will be seen, then, that the Hebrew law does no
small or common thing for the Slave when it makes
him a member of the Congregation, and expressly enjoins that he shall take part with the freeman in the
most solemn acts of national worship. "And thou
shalt keep the feast of weeks unto the Lord thy God
with a tribute of a freewill offering of thine hand,
which thou shalt give unto the Lord thy God, according as the Lord thy God hath blessed thee: and thou
shalt rejoice before the Lord thy God, thou, and thy
son, and thy daughter, *and thy manservant, and thy
maidservant*, and the Levite that is within thy gates,
and the stranger, and the fatherless, and the widow,
that are among you, in the place which the Lord thy
God hath chosen to place His name there. And thou
shalt remember that *thou wast a bondman* in Egypt:

men, should wear chaplets and rest (στεφανηφορεῖν καὶ ἐλινύειν) on a certain day: but this is little more than loosing the ox from the plough.

and thou shalt observe and do these statutes. Thou shalt observe the feast of tabernacles seven days, after that thou hast gathered in thy corn and thy wine: and thou shalt rejoice in thy feast, thou, and thy son, and thy daughter, and *thy manservant*, and *thy maidservant*, and the Levite, the stranger, and the fatherless, and the widow, that are within thy gates. Seven days shalt thou keep a solemn feast unto the Lord thy God in the place which the Lord shall choose: because the Lord thy God shall bless thee in all thine increase, and in all the works of thine hands, therefore thou shalt surely rejoice. Three times in a year shall *all thy males* appear before the Lord thy God in the place which He shall choose; in the feast of unleavened bread, and in the feast of weeks, and in the feast of tabernacles: and they shall not appear before the Lord empty: every man shall give as he is able, according to the blessing of the Lord thy God which He hath given thee[n]."

The bondman came up to stand with the freeman before the Lord. The gift of the bondman was mingled with that of the freeman, and was equally accepted. Perfect religious equality was thus proclaimed, and that in a Commonwealth of which religion was the foundation, and of which Jehovah was King. No cruel division of classes, no aristocratic pride on one side, or degradation on the other, could well hold its ground against such a law.

The place of the festival is to be "that which the Lord shall choose;" and to that place the bond-

[n] Deut. xvi. 10—17.

man is to come, whatever inconvenience his absence from home may cause to his master: the interests of the master being in this case, as in the case of the Sabbath, set aside with a high hand in favour of the slave's interest as a moral being, and of the claims of religion.

And the bondman of a priest ministering in holy things was not to be a mere "slave of the temple." Whatever measure of sanctity attached to the rest of the priest's household was to attach also to him. "There shall no stranger eat of the holy thing: a sojourner of the priest or an hired servant shall not eat of the holy thing. But if the priest buy any soul with his money, he shall eat of it, and he that is born in his house: they shall eat of his meat[o]."

Still more momentous perhaps than the ordinance which makes the slave a partaker with the rest of the nation in its public worship, is the ordinance which makes him a partaker with the rest of the family in the Passover:—"This is the ordinance of the Passover: There shall no stranger eat thereof: but every man's servant that is bought for money, when thou hast circumcised him, then shall he eat thereof[p]." The Lawgiver goes on to enact that "a foreigner and an hired servant shall not eat thereof;" as though to make it clear that the reason why the bondman is to partake is that he is in the fullest sense a member of the family. No one could eat of the passover who had not been circumcised; but, as we have seen before, the head of a family was required by the command originally given to Abraham to circumcise all his household, "whether

[o] Levit. xxii. 10.   [p] Exod. xii. 43.

born in his house or bought with his money q." And "in the selfsame day was Abraham circumcised, and Ishmael his son. And all the men of his house, born in the house, and bought with money of the stranger, were circumcised with him." The servants whom Abraham had bought with his money must have been strangers to his blood and that of his tribe. We know that in heathen communities, during the early period of their history, membership of the community depended on kinship by blood, real or traditional. A certain number of Families or Houses, the members of which claimed a common ancestor, made up the Tribe, and a certain number of Tribes made up the Commonwealth. When the circle was first enlarged, it was by adoption. Not to be a member of a family and tribe was to be a political outcast r. The families or houses were bound together by religious rites, participation in which was the sign and test of membership. Primitive Rome was the most striking type of this order of things. But primitive Athens also afforded an instance of it. In the same way the Hebrew Commonwealth, in the time of Moses, consists of families or houses, grouped into tribes, the family and the tribe alike being the offspring of a common ancestor. In the Numbering of the people they are taken by their tribes, and then numbered " by their generations, after their families, by the house of their fathers." The family or house is the elementary group and the basis of the whole. " It may be affirmed," says Professor

---

q Gen. xvii. 13.
r ἀφρήτωρ, ἀθέμιστος, ἀνέστιος, ὗς ἑπτέτης ὢν οὐκ ἔφυσε φράτορας.

Maine[s], "of early commonwealths, that their citizens considered all the groups in which they claimed membership to be founded on common lineage." "The history of political ideas," says the same writer, "begins in fact with the assumption that kinship in blood is the sole possible ground of community in political functions; nor is there any of those subversions of feeling which we emphatically term revolutions, so startling and so complete as the change which is accomplished when some other principle—such as that, for instance, of *local contiguity*—establishes itself for the first time as the basis of common political action." The revolution of which Professor Maine here speaks was effected both at Rome and at Athens by struggles between the men of the privileged lineage and those who were strangers to it, which shook the Commonwealth to its centre: and the family rites, from their hereditary character, were a stronghold of exclusion, and made religion a source of division and injustice in the State.

Among the Hebrews, the rite of circumcision administered to all alike, and the participation of the whole household in the family rite of the Passover, combined with the law requiring the presence of all males at the solemn seasons before the Lord, effectually incorporated even the foreign slave into the community, without doing violence to the ideas on which, at that period, society was necessarily based.

The fitness of the Passover especially for this great

[s] Ancient Law, p. 129.

social purpose is very striking. It stands in marked contrast not only to the mock association of the slave with the master in the Saturnalia, but to sacrifices offered by the head of a family as its priest on behalf of the household. It is a holy meal at which the master must eat with the slave: its religious meaning is such as to secure that participation in it shall be a serious bond: it links together all who partake in it, by the memory of the most solemn event in the national history, to the destinies of the nation: it recalls the time when all the members of that nation were alike bondmen of the stranger in a foreign land. Never, surely, did Providence so thwart its own design, if the design of Providence was to widen and perpetuate the distinction between the freeman and the slave.

In America the slave is made a Christian in a sense of which we may have more to say hereafter. But practically he can scarcely be said to belong to the same Church any more than to the same State with his master. He sometimes sits in a separate part of the same place of worship, and receives the Communion separately from the same hands. But generally speaking, his religious exercises are carried on apart in his own quarters. Mr. Olmsted says, that "though family prayers were held in several of the fifty planters' houses in Mississippi and Alabama, in which he passed a night, he never in a single instance saw a field-hand attend, or join in the devotion of the family[t]." A friend of the present writer staying in the house of a planter who

[t] A Journ-y in the Back Country, p. 108.

was a religious man, was surprised to find that the servants did not come to prayers [u].

Slavery, in Greece and at Rome, may in the earliest times have been a social necessity and a sound relation, as it was in the Patriarchal East. But in more civilized times it became a manifest wrong: and then theories were invented to appease the moral misgivings of the slave-owners by shewing that the wrong which conduced so much to their advantage, when viewed by the eye of reason, was the perfection of right [v]. The philosophic Greek feigned that there were certain races of men doomed by their natural inferiority to be the slaves of the superior race; and among the races so doomed he included some which were of the same stock as himself, and certainly would have included those which have become the founders of modern civilization [x]. The

---

[u] If I am told that the negroes are treated, in the matter of public worship or in other matters, as a Pariah class in the North as well as in the South, I must answer that the thing here discussed is not the consistency of the North, but the validity of a plea for slavery put forward by the South. I may add that the degradation inflicted by slavery in the South must naturally cling to the negro, except in the eyes of very high-minded men, in the North. Further, I would ask, are those who maltreat the negro in the North the enemies or the friends of slavery? And if they are the enemies of slavery, is their conduct the consequence of their principles or a departure from them?

[v] See Maine's Ancient Law, p. 162.

[x] A gentleman who was among my audience at Manchester, and has done me the honour to send me some criticisms on the lecture, complains that I did not notice the inferiority of the negro race, which seems to him to be "a matter of fact" greatly affecting the question. The inferiority of the negro cannot be more manifest to him, than *his* inferiority and the consequent propriety of making *him* a slave would have been to Aristotle, the father of natural science. What race would not be "inferior" while it was kept in a state of degradation?

Roman, a soldier and a lawyer, pretended that servitude was the ransom paid by the vanquished for a life legally forfeited to the victor in war. The American Slave-owner, since he has cast off shame, and embraced as good that which he once excused as a transient evil, has borrowed the theory of the Greek; and he has so far improved upon it as to assert that a negro is not a man[y]: an assertion which, if he really believed it, would take away a shade of darkness from his cruelty only to add a deeper shade of darkness to his lust. All these theories tend to ratify the degradation of the slave, and those which describe his lot as an ordinance of nature tend to make it unchangeable and hopeless. But in the Old Testament we have no theory or suggestion of the kind. On the contrary, the Hebrew master is often reminded that he was himself brought "out of the house of bondage," and adjured, by that remembrance, to love mercy and do justice.

Did the Hebrew Lawgiver encourage, or did he discourage, the multiplication of Slaves? We have seen already that he provided for the constant reduction of their number by requiring that every Hebrew bond-

---

[y] "The wide-spread delusion that Southern institutions are an evil, and their extension dangerous—the notion so prevalent at the North that there is a real antagonism, or that the system of the South is hostile to Northern interests; the weakened Union sentiment, and the utter debauchment, the absolute traitorism of a portion of the Northern people, not only to the Union but to Democratic institutions and to the cause of civilization on this Continent; all these with the minor and most innumerable mischiefs that this mighty world-wide imposture has engendered or drags in its midst, rest upon the dogma, the single assumption, the sole elementary foundation falsehood, that a negro is a black man."

man should be set free in the seventh year, and that, if he had brought a wife and children with him into bondage, he should take them out with him. This, however, is not all. We may reckon four principal sources from which the nations of antiquity derived their slaves : (1) Conquest, which was the greatest source of all; (2) Piracy and kidnapping, which was a great source of slaves in early times among the Greeks, and in later times at Rome; (3) Penal servitude for crime, which was a less but still a considerable source; (4) Debt, which, under harsh laws, made the debtor, in default of payment, the slave of the creditor. The early period of Roman history is filled, as is well known, with the troubles caused by the cruelty of creditors, who, having lent money to the poor at usurious interest, seized for the debt the property, the families, and the persons of their insolvent debtors. This was in fact the source of a desperate conflict between classes, ending in a great political revolution. The same thing took place in Attica, where multitudes of the peasant proprietors, overwhelmed with debts contracted by borrowing money of the rich at a high rate of interest, had not only lost their holdings, which they had mortgaged for the money, but were themselves being sold into slavery; till at last affairs came to a desperate crisis, and the government was put, with extraordinary powers, into the hands of Solon, who could only cure the evil by a moderate use of the sponge. The lower orders in ancient Gaul had been in like manner reduced by debt to become bondmen to the nobility when the Romans entered the country, and there can be little doubt that this degradation of the mass of the people must have aided the arms of the invader. The Hebrew nation was liable to the same evil. "Now there cried a certain woman of the wives of the sons of the prophets unto Elisha, saying, Thy servant my husband is dead ... and the creditor is come to take unto him my two sons to be bondmen[z]."

Now (1) as to war, we have seen that the Hebrew Lawgiver, without forbidding war, practically discouraged it; and that he almost prohibited conquest by prohibiting the means of it, forced service in war, and a standing army of chariots and horsemen[a]: (2) as to kidnapping, he enacts that not only the stealer of a man, but the receiver of a man who has been stolen, shall be punished with death[b]: (3) as to penal servitude, we have seen the single instance in

[z] 2 Kings iv. 1.

[a] That is, of course, when they had once conquered the land of Canaan. And, as the Canaanites were to be destroyed, this conquest would not be a source of slaves, like those of the Dorians and other tribes who reduced the old inhabitants of the conquered country to bondage. This is not the place to discuss the tremendous moral questions connected with the penal destruction of the Canaanites. But it may be remarked that had they been spared and reduced to slavery, the result, judging from analogy, would have been the deep corruption of the Chosen People. With abundance of slave labour, the Jews would not have taken to industry, nor have acquired the virtues which industry alone can produce and guard. Their fate would have been like that of the Turks and other conquering hordes of the East, which, the rush of conquest once over, not being forced to labour, have sunk into mere sloth and abject sensuality. And if the morals of the Canaanites are truly painted in the Pentateuch, the possession of such slaves would have been depraving in the highest degree.

[b] "And he that stealeth a man, and selleth him, or if he be found in his hand, he shall surely be put to death."—Exod. xxi. 16.

which he prescribes it, his general penalties for secondary offences being fines and corporal punishment: and (4) he absolutely forbids the lending of money upon usury to a brother in want, the source of the debts which crushed the Attic and Roman peasantry, and caused them and their families to become slaves. "If thou lend money to any of My people that is poor by thee, thou shalt not be to him as an usurer, neither shalt thou lay upon him usury [c]." " And if thy brother be waxen poor, and fallen in decay with thee; then thou shalt relieve him: yea, though he be a stranger, or a sojourner; that he may live with thee. Take thou no usury of him, or increase: but fear thy God; that thy brother may live with thee. Thou shalt not give him thy money upon usury, nor lend him thy victuals for increase. I am the Lord your God, which brought you forth out of the land of Egypt, to give you the land of Canaan, and to be your God[d]." Laws against usury are absurd in the present state of society. But in the state of society with which the Hebrew Lawgiver had to deal, they might, as we learn from the example of Greece and Rome, be the salvation of the people.

The first step towards the enslaving of the peasant's person at Rome and Athens was the mortgaging and forfeiture of his little plot of land. Against this likewise the Hebrew lawgiver guards. "The land shall not be sold for ever: for the land is Mine; for ye are strangers and sojourners with Me. And in all the land of your possession ye shall grant a redemption for the land. If thy brother be waxen poor, and hath sold away

[c] Exod. xxii. 25.   [d] Levit. xxv. 35—38.

some of his possession, and if any of his kin come to redeem it, then shall he redeem that which his brother sold. And if the man have none to redeem it, and himself be able to redeem it; then let him count the years of the sale thereof, and restore the overplus unto the man to whom he sold it; that he may return unto his possession. But if he be not able to restore it to him, then that which is sold shall remain in the hand of him that hath bought it until the year of jubile: and in the jubile it shall go out, and he shall return unto his possession[e]."

This law, like that against retaining a brother in bondage, though not regularly observed, did not become a dead letter. We have its practical effect in Nehemiah, ch. v.: "And there was a great cry of the people and of their wives against their brethren the Jews. For there were that said, We, our sons, and our daughters, are many: therefore we take up corn for them, that we may eat, and live. Some also there were that said, We have mortgaged our lands, vineyards, and houses, that we might buy corn, because of the dearth. There were also that said, We have borrowed money for the King's tribute, and that upon our lands and vineyards. Yet now our flesh is as the flesh of our brethren, our children as their children: and, lo, we bring into bondage our sons and our daughters to be servants, and some of our daughters are brought into bondage already: neither is it in our power to redeem them; for other men have our lands and vineyards. And I was very angry when I heard their cry and these

[e] Levit. xxv. 23—28.

words. Then I consulted with myself, and I rebuked the nobles, and the rulers, and said unto them, Ye exact usury, every one of his brother. And I set a great assembly against them. And I said unto them, We after our ability have redeemed our brethren the Jews, which were sold unto the heathen; and will ye even sell your brethren? or shall they be sold unto us? Then held they their peace, and found nothing to answer. Also I said, It is not good that ye do: ought ye not to walk in the fear of our God because of the reproach of the heathen our enemies? I likewise, and my brethren, and my servants, might expect of them money and corn: I pray you, let us leave off this usury. Restore, I pray you, to them, even this day, their lands, their vineyards, their oliveyards, and their houses, also the hundredth part of the money, and of the corn, the wine, and the oil, that ye exact of them. Then said they, We will restore them, and will require nothing of them; so will we do as thou sayest."

The Hebrew Lawgiver founds a people of peasant proprietors, among whom the land is equally divided. Such seemed the surest way of producing a moral, religious, and patriotic nation. And the paramount object of the property law is to preserve these peasant proprietors, and prevent their homesteads from being engrossed, as the homesteads of the peasant proprietors in Italy were engrossed, by the rich capitalists, "who join house to house and lay field to field, till there be no place, that they may be placed alone in the midst of the earth." "The Land is Mine" warns off the cupidity of the capitalist, and places each little inheritance under the guardianship of God. But a system of small properties is not only adverse, but fatal, to slave culture, which can be profitably carried on only by large gangs of slaves working upon great estates, like the Roman *latifundia* or the plantations of the South.

The interests of the free labourer are guarded with as much care as that of the small proprietor. "Thou shalt not defraud thy neighbour, neither rob him: the wages of him that is hired shall not abide with thee all night until the morning[f]." "Thou shalt not oppress an hired servant that is poor and needy, whether he be of thy brethren, or of thy strangers that are in thy land within thy gates: at his day thou shalt give him his hire, neither shall the sun go down upon it; for he is poor, and setteth his heart upon it: lest he cry against thee unto the Lord, and it be sin unto thee[g]." The spirit of these precepts lived in the nation. Jeremiah denounces "Woe unto him that buildeth his house by unrighteousness, and his chambers by wrong; that useth his neighbour's service without wages, and giveth him not for his work[h]." And so in Malachi (iii. 5), "I will come near to you to judgment; and I will be a swift witness against the sorcerers, and against the adulterers, and against false swearers, *and against those that oppress the hireling in his wages*, the widow, and the fatherless, and that turn aside the stranger from his right, and fear not Me, saith the Lord of hosts." To "use your neighbour's service without wages," and

[f] Levit. xix. 13.   [g] Deut. xxiv. 14, 15.   [h] Jer. xxii. 13.

thereby degrade the free labourer into a serf, was the practice of feudal kings and tyrants as well as of the Oriental despots round Judæa. The Statutes of Labourers passed by the feudal Parliaments of England to compel the Labourer to serve at old rates in spite of a rise 'in prices and in the value of labour, were an instance of a kind of oppression which has widely prevailed when the lower classes have been in the power of the higher. And these parts of the Mosaic law are not to be read as vague moral precepts or general sentiments, but as specific provisions pointed against the besetting evils of society in that age.

The following law also shews the most tender and touching care for the interests, and even for the dignity, of the poor man: "When thou dost lend thy brother anything, thou shalt not go into his house to fetch his pledge. Thou shalt stand abroad, and the man to whom thou dost lend shall bring out the pledge abroad unto thee. And if the man be poor, thou shalt not sleep with his pledge: in any case thou shalt deliver him the pledge again when the sun goeth down, that he may sleep in his own raiment, and bless thee: and it shall be righteousness unto thee before the Lord thy God[1]."

"If there be among you a poor man of one of thy brethren within any of thy gates in thy land which the Lord thy God giveth thee, thou shalt not harden thine heart, nor shut thine hand from thy poor brother: but thou shalt open thine hand wide unto him, and shalt surely lend him sufficient for his need, in

[1] Deut. xxiv. 10—13.

that which he wanteth. Beware that there be not a thought in thy wicked heart, saying, The seventh year, the year of release, is at hand; and thine eye be evil against thy poor brother, and thou givest him nought; and he cry unto the Lord against thee, and it be sin unto thee. Thou shalt surely give him, and thine heart shall not be grieved when thou givest unto him: because that for this thing the Lord thy God shall bless thee in all thy works, and in all that thou puttest thine hand unto. For the poor shall never cease out of the land: therefore I command thee, saying, Thou shalt open thine hand wide unto thy brother, to thy poor, and to thy needy, in thy land[k]." This and the like precepts of charity and liberality all tend not only to save the poor from the destitution which led to bondage, but to throw round their persons a religious sanctity which would guard them from the indignity of being made serfs or slaves. The same is the tendency of the injunctions in favour of the gleaner : "When thou cuttest down thine harvest in thy field, and hast forgot a sheaf in the field, thou shalt not go again to fetch it: it shall be for the stranger, for the fatherless, and for the widow: that the Lord thy God may bless thee in all the work of thine hands. When thou beatest thine olive tree, thou shalt not go over the boughs again: it shall be for the stranger, for the fatherless, and for the widow. When thou gatherest the grapes of thy vineyard, thou shalt not glean it afterward : it shall be for the stranger, for the fatherless, and for the widow. And thou shalt

[k] Deut. xv. 7—11.

remember that thou wast a bondman in the land of Egypt: therefore I command thee to do this thing[1]."

The ordinance requiring the appointment of regular judges throughout the nation, and enjoining them to "judge righteously between every man and his brother," "not to respect persons in judgment," "not to be afraid of the face of man, for the judgment is God's," would also, besides its more obvious benefit, tend to preserve the independence of the poor; since it assured them the protection of the law in place of the protection of great men, which in unsettled and dangerous times they are tempted to purchase, and in the early feudal period did habitually purchase, at the price of their personal liberty.

"Let our Legislature," says *The Southern Democrat*, "pass a law that whoever will take these parents, (parents unable to educate their children out of their own pockets,) and take care of them and their offspring, in sickness and in health, clothe them, feed them, and house them, shall be legally entitled to their services." "We have got," says the same journal, "to hating everything with the prefix free, from free negroes up and down through the whole catalogue, free farms, free labour, free society, free will, free thinking, and free schools. But the worst of all these abominations is the modern system of free schools." "We have asked the North," says *The Richmond Inquirer*, "has not the experiment of universal liberty failed, are not the evils of free society insufferable? Still no answer. Their universal silence is a conclusive proof, added to

---

[1] Deut. xxiv. 19—22.

many others we have furnished, that free society in the long run is an impracticable form of society. It is everywhere starving, demoralizing, and insurrectionary. Policy and humanity alike forbid the extension of the evils of free society to new people and coming generations." Free society, according to a kindred authority, is nothing but "a conglomeration of greasy mechanics, filthy operatives, small-fisted farmers, and moonstruck theorists."

It appears that the author of the Hebrew Law was not of this opinion. It appears from his enactments that he did not think free labour, to use the phrase of another Southern writer, " the great cancer" and " the offensive fungus" of civilized society[m], though he was as well aware as any advocate of Slavery that the lot of the free labourer was precarious, and that the poor would be always in the land.

[m] "The institution of slavery operates by contrast and comparison; it elevates the tone of the superior, adds to its (*sic*) refinement, allows more time to cultivate the mind, exalts the standard in morals, manners, and intellectual endowments; operates as a safety valve for the evil-disposed, leaving the upper race purer, while it really preserves from degradation, in the scale of civilization, the inferior, which we see is their uniform destiny when left to themselves. The slaves constitute essentially the lowest class, and society is immeasurably benefited by having this class, which constitutes the offensive fungus, the great cancer of civilized life—a vast burden and expense to every community—under surveillance and control; and not only so, but under direction as an efficient agent to promote the general welfare and increase the wealth of the community. The history of the world furnishes no institution under similar management, where so much good actually results to the governors and the governed as this in the Southern States of North America."—From an *Address on Climatology*, before the Academy of 'Science, by Dr. Barton of New Orleans, quoted by Mr. Olmsted, *Journeys and Explorations*, vol. ii. p. 277.

In one thing, however, the American Slave-owner and the Hebrew Lawgiver are agreed. Both think, and with good reason, that Slavery and Free Labour cannot well exist together. The Hebrew Lawgiver therefore takes measures to diminish Slavery in his country. The American Slave-owner proposes to put an end to the freedom of labour all over the world.

There is one thing more to be mentioned. Decisive experience has shewn that Slavery cannot hold its ground without a fugitive slave law. Now the law of Moses says, "Thou shalt not deliver unto his master the servant which is escaped from his master unto thee: He shall dwell with thee, even among you, in that place which he shall choose in one of thy gates, where it liketh him best: thou shalt not oppress him[n]." Southern theologians try to get rid of the apparent immorality of this passage by maintaining that it relates only to slaves who have fled from a foreign country. It is difficult to see any ground for this gloss, more especially as even in heathen Greece the right of asylum in certain temples was allowed, alone of religious privileges, to the slave. But suppose it were so, the law would in effect enjoin the Hebrews to risk a quarrel and perhaps a war with a foreign country rather than give up fugitive slaves. A singular mode of impressing the sanctity and beneficence of Slavery on their minds.

Lastly, let us ask what was the practical effect of the Mosaic legislation in the matter of Slavery? Was the nation of Moses a Slave Power?

[n] Deut. xxiii. 15, 16.

The social marks of a Slave State lie on the surface. At Athens we have the slaves running away by thousands to an invader when he takes post in the country. We have the slaves in the mines of Laurium rising, seizing the fortress of Sunium, and holding out there against their masters. At Sparta we have the servile population taking advantage of an earthquake to break out in desperate insurrection; and on another occasion the government takes off by secret assassination two thousand Helots, whose valour, displayed in its own military service, it sees reason to fear[o]. At Rome we have a series of the most sanguinary servile wars; and after the final victory of the masters the road from Rome to Capua is garnished with sixteen thousand crosses, on which writhe the bodies of the vanquished slaves. The serfdom of the Middle Ages was signalized by the Jacquerie, the Peasants' War, and the revolt of the English villains under Wat Tyler. There were frequent disturbances among the slaves in our West Indian colonies. There was a dreadful insurrection in St. Domingo. There have been insurrections in the Southern States; and the panics caused by them among the whites have led to cruel reigns of terror[p].

[o] Thucyd. iv. 80.
[p] One of these reigns of terror is thus described by a slave:—"It was a grand opportunity for the low whites, who had no negroes of their own to scourge. They exulted in such a chance to exercise a little brief authority, and shew their subserviency to the slave-holders; not reflecting that the power which trampled on the coloured people also kept themselves in poverty, ignorance, and moral degradation. Those who never witnessed such scenes can hardly believe what I know was inflicted at this time on innocent men, women, and children, against whom there was not the slightest ground for suspicion. Coloured people

Not only so, but over Slave States there has always brooded an atmosphere charged with the fear which springs from the consciousness of a great wrong. The laws and customs of Sparta, for fear of the Helots, were those of a city in a perpetual state of siege. Whatever may have been the exact nature of the Crypteia, it certainly was an instrument of terrorism put in action each year against the servile class. Plato himself, when, not without a deep moral pang, he has acquiesced in the necessity of Slavery, sanctions the inhuman policy of mixing together as much as possible slaves of different races and languages, that they may not be able to communicate and conspire with each other. This policy, and that of encouraging

---

and slaves who lived in remote parts of the town suffered in an especial manner. In some cases the searchers scattered powder and shot among their clothes, and then sent other parties to find them, and bring them forward as proof that they were plotting insurrection. Everywhere men, women, and children were whipped till the blood stood in puddles at their feet. Some received five hundred lashes; others were tied hands and feet, and tortured with a bucking paddle, which blisters the skin terribly. The dwellings of the coloured people, unless they happened to be protected by some influential white person, who was nigh at hand, were robbed of clothing and every thing else the marauders thought worth carrying away. All day long these unfeeling wretches went round, like a troop of demons, terrifying and tormenting the helpless. At night, they formed themselves into patrol bands, and went wherever they chose among the coloured people, acting out their brutal will. Many women hid themselves in woods and swamps, to keep out of their way. If any of the husbands or fathers told of these outrages, they were tied up to the public whipping-post, and cruelly scourged for telling lies about white men. The consternation was universal. No two people that had the slightest tinge of colour in their faces dared to be seen talking together."—*The Deeper Wrong; or, Incidents in the Life of a Slave Girl. Written by Herself. Edited by L. Maria Child*, pp. 98, 99.

dissensions among them, were in fact parts of the economic system of antiquity. The Roman was, as usual, plain in his sentiments and practical in his measures. "So many slaves," he said, "so many enemies;" and it was a maxim of the Roman writers on agriculture that "a good watch-dog ought not to be on too friendly terms with his fellow-slaves." The Senate feared to let the slaves wear the same dress, lest they should become conscious of their own numbers. If a master was found dead, every slave in the household was at once and without trial put to death: and the number of victims on one occasion to this horrible safeguard of tyranny was no less than four hundred. Of the relations in which the feudal lords as a class stood to their serfs, the Statute-book of the later Plantagenets and the earlier Tudors is the record. In the Southern States the law forbids the education of slaves, a precaution which goes beyond the cruel fear of the Roman slave-owner; for at Rome not only was the education of slaves freely permitted, but many of them received the highest education, and were employed in callings of the most intellectual kind. The jealousy of the police in the Slave States, as described by Mr. Olmsted [q], also marks the constant presence of a great social danger. "In Richmond, and Charleston, and New Orleans," says that writer, "the citizens are as careless and as gay as in Boston or London, and their servants a thousand times as childlike and cordial to all appearance, in their relations with them, as our servants are with us. But go to the bottom of this

[q] A Journey to the Back Country, p. 443.

security and dependence, and you come to police machinery, such as you never find in towns under free government; citadels, sentries, passports, grape-shotted cannon, and daily public whippings of the subjects for accidental infractions of police ceremonies. I happened myself to see more direct expression of tyranny in a single day and night at Charleston than at Naples in a week; and I found that more than half the inhabitants of this town were subject to arrest, imprisonment, and barbarous punishment, if found in the streets without a passport after the evening gun-fire. Similar precautions and similar customs may be discovered in every larger town in the South." Mr. Olmsted says that it is not in reality much better in the rural districts: that the apparent freedom of the slaves in those districts is the apparent freedom of convicts in a dockyard, an armed force, invested with more arbitrary and cruel power than any police in Europe, being always ready to act if not always in service. He adds that the security of the whites, however, depends less on the patrols than on the instinctive, habitual, and constant surveillance exercised by all the whites over all the blacks. He has seen a gentleman without commission or authority oblige negroes to shew their passports, merely because he did not recognise them as belonging to any of his neighbours. He has seen a white girl, twelve years old, stop a black man on the public road, demand to know whither he was going, and by whose authority, order him back to his plantation, and when he demurred, threaten to have him whipped. Fear has even driven the American Slave-owners into practices which rival in cruelty the Roman practice of crucifying slaves. A slave who had killed his master "was roasted alive at a slow fire on the spot of the murder, in the presence of many thousand slaves, driven to the ground from all the adjoining counties; and when at length his life went out, the fire was intensified until his body was in ashes, which were scattered to the winds and trampled under foot[r]." Mr. Olmsted gives the words of newspapers, even newspapers which from their moderation lie under the reproach of abolitionism, justifying such burnings of negroes as acts at once deliberate and indispensable. One editor, a Methodist preacher, says, "that the punishment was unequal to the crime, and that, had he been there, he would have suggested that the negro should be torn limb from limb with red-hot pincers, and that the limbs should afterwards have been burnt in a heap." The burning of slaves alive, as well as crucifixion, was a part of the system of terror practised by the Romans[s]. The American master, it is said, sleeps with open doors. So did the Roman master: his guards were the vengeance of his class, the stake and the cross.

In the First Book of Kings (i. 39), two of the servants of Shimei run away to Achish, King of Gath. This, it is believed, is the sum total of the slave disturbances recorded in the annals of the Hebrew nation. The churlish Nabal, to excuse himself for refusing hospitality to David and his followers, pretends to believe

[r] Olmsted, Journey to the Back Woods, p. 443.
[s] Plaut., Capt., III. iv. 65.

that they may be runaway servants, for "there be many servants now a days that break away every man from his master." But when we inquire who were with David in the cave of Adullam, we find that they were men "in distress," "in debt," and "discontented," not runaway slaves[t].

The economical marks of a Slave State are almost as clear as its political marks. "The great plantations," (*latifundia*,) says a Roman writer, "have ruined Italy, and they are ruining the provinces too." "Slave labour," says Pliny, "makes bad husbandry, like everything that is done by despair[u]." Within sixty years after the death of Constantine, Campania, once the garden of Italy, was surveyed by the government, and an exemption from taxes was granted in favour of three hundred and thirty thousand acres of desert land. "As the footsteps of the barbarians," says Gibbon, "had not yet been seen in Italy, the cause of this amazing desolation which is recorded in the laws, can be ascribed only to the administration of the Roman Emperors." A blight more deadly to the fruitfulness of the land than that of imperial administration had been there. In America, as is well known, Slavery subsists by moving forwards to fresh soil, and it leaves a desert, like that of ruined Campania, where it has been. But the land of the Hebrews appears to have been cultivated with a care which carried fertility to the hill-

[t] 1 Sam. xxii. 2. The manservants and maidservants of the people, on their return from the Captivity, were in number 7,337. (Nehem. vii. 67.)

[u] "Coli rura ab ergastulis pessimum est, et quicquid agitur a desperantibus."

tops, and which bespeaks not only free labour, but the love of a peasant proprietor for his own land.

Solomon imposed, for his great works generally, a tribute of bond-service on the nations of alien blood which were under his sway[v]. But to build the Temple, he raised a great levy out of all Israel[x]: and it must have been a levy of freemen, since we are expressly told that "of the children of Israel Solomon made no bondmen." It is not probable, then, that he had a great amount of slave labour at his command. Nor, though his palaces were great and costly, did he or his successors indulge in Pyramids, Labyrinths, Towers of Belus, or any of those wasteful freaks of despotic architecture which a great command of slave labour naturally inspires. The description of the Temple, grand and sumptuous, but without anything colossal or monstrous, bespeaks the work of freedom, which spares labour and seeks effect, not by magnitude, but by art[y]. When the Temple is repaired, under Josiah, the work is done by free labourers receiving wages. "Go up to Hilkiah the high priest, that he may sum the silver which is brought into the house of the Lord, which the keepers of the door have gathered of the people: and let them deliver it into the hand of the doers of the work, that have the oversight of the house of the Lord: and let them give it to the doers of the

[v] 1 Kings ix. 21.   [x] Ibid. v. 13.

[y] The taste of the Greeks would probably have preserved them from colossal extravagance in art under any circumstances; but it is not probable that, at the time when the type of Greek architecture was fixed, the nation possessed many slaves.

work which is in the house of the Lord, to repair the breaches of the house[z]."

There is not, it is believed, in the Hebrew annals any trace of the existence of a slave-market, nor anything else indicating a trade in slaves. Sion, therefore, probably presented no counterpart to the auctions and advertisements of the South.

In Slave States labour is always looked upon by freemen as a degradation. No Spartan would have thought of engaging in any work but war. Even at Athens, which was much less of a Slave State than Sparta, the name mechanic was, as in nations infected with feudal sentiments, a term of reproach[a]. The poor freeman at Rome despised labour, and lived by selling his suffrage at elections, by sponging on a rich patron, and by the dole which he received out of the tribute paid by the provinces to the conquering people. No member, however indigent, of a feudal aristocracy would have stooped to touch a plough. The poor whites of the South in like manner refuse to do the same work as the negro, and subsist as dependants of the great planters, or by occupations which, however wretched and precarious, are not those of the slave. There is not a trace of any such sentiment in the records of the Hebrew nation, any more than in those of its patriarchal sires. On the contrary, every mention of labour indicates that it was had in honour. "Blessed is every one that feareth the Lord; that walketh in His ways. For thou shalt eat the labour of thine hands: happy shalt thou be, and well shall it be with

[z] 2 Kings xxii. 4, 5.   [a] οὐ γὰρ βάναυσον τὴν τέχνην ἐκτησάμην, &c.

thee." "Wealth gotten by vanity shall be diminished: but he that gathereth by labour shall increase." "And also that every man should eat and drink, and enjoy the good of all his labour, it is the gift of God." Not only the honoured founders of the nation, as we have said, but its heroes, kings, and prophets were sons of labour, and had taken part in the work of that class which American Slave-owners call the fungus and cancer of society. Gideon, when the angel of the Lord appeared to him, was threshing wheat by the winepress[b]. Saul was in search of his father's asses when he was anointed king of Israel. David was taken from following the flocks. Elisha was called from the plough. Amos was a herdsman.

The spirit of a slave-owning aristocracy is insolent, as we know by the example of Lacedæmon and of the Southern States. But that of slave-owners under a despotism is doubly slavish, as we know by the example of Imperial Rome. The spirit of the Hebrew people in its dealings with its kings is high and free. Solomon in all his power does not dare to treat them as bondmen, and they at once break the yoke of his tyrant son. Their undying patriotism, their unfailing hope for their country, the tenacity of national life which brings them back from Babylon and restores their Commonwealth and Temple, would never, it may safely be said, have been found in a Slave State. Nothing of the kind was shewn even by the indomitable Roman when once his character had been corrupted by the possession of wealth and a multitude of slaves.

[b] Judges vi. 11.

The hearts of the Hebrews were "hard." In matters of social humanity and justice they fell away from the beneficent precepts of their lawgiver in their dealings with their neighbour, as in matters of religion they fell away from their allegiance to the true God. Judaism was not Christianity, nor was Judæa Christendom; yet it may perhaps be safely said, that no two communities in the history of the world have been more different from each other than the community of great capitalists and landowners with their droves of slaves which covers the Southern States of America, and the community of peasants "dwelling each under his own vine and his own fig-tree," and each "going forth to his labour until the evening," which in the happy days of the Hebrew people lay around the Holy City and worshipped together in the Courts of Sion. It was among this peasantry, true sons of labour yet free of soul, pure, simple-minded, religious, and though devoid of the wisdom of the world, not uninstructed in religion, that when the time for the fulfilment of their long-cherished hope was come, the Saviour of the world appeared. It was from their cottages and fishing-boats that He called the open and ardent natures, neither corrupted by riches nor debased by Slavery, which were destined to confront a world in the strength of conviction, and to become the founders of Christendom.

SECTION IV.

THE New Testament is not concerned with any political or social institutions: for political and social institutions belong to particular nations and particular phases of society. But now the fulness of time is come. Greek and Roman conquest and Greek intellect have conspired together to break down the exclusive barriers of narrow nationality. Upon the more exalted minds the great truth of the universal brotherhood of man has begun to dawn, and Cicero has advanced far enough to see that the universe "is one great commonwealth of gods and men." The gods of the nations have been overthrown, and have left the hearts of men open and craving for a new faith. The Jewish religion itself has burst its bounds and become active in conversion. Therefore the expectation of Israel and of the world is fulfilled. The universal religion arrives. The Chosen People having done its appointed work in preparing the way for the Messiah, merges in the people of believers throughout the world. The family which ate of the Passover opens out into the Household of Faith. The Son of David is the Son of Man.

We shall hear no more, then, of social and political reforms, such as Moses introduced by his code into the laws and customs of the Hebrew nation. Whatever is done will be done for the whole of mankind and for all time. The present will be sacrificed without hesitation to the future. If it be necessary for the eternal purpose of the Gospel, the Apostle will submit to all the injustice of heathen governments, and receive martyrdom at the hand of a Nero. If it be necessary for the same purpose, the slave of a heathen master will patiently remain a slave.

Nothing indeed marks the divine character of the Gospel more than its perfect freedom from any appeal to the spirit of political revolution. The Founder of Christianity and His Apostles were surrounded by everything which could tempt human reformers to enter on revolutionary courses. Their nation was grievously oppressed and shamefully degraded. The rulers and princes of Judæa were sensual and cruel tyrants; and their tyranny was supported by a central tyranny, equally cruel and sensual, which had its seat at Rome. Injustice in the form of Pilate sate on the judgment-seat. A foreign soldiery filled the land, "doing violence," "accusing men falsely," "not content with their wages;" and, what was worse than all, stalking in the arrogance of conquest over the burning hearts of the Chosen People. So oppressive was the fiscal system that the name of a collector of the taxes was a byeword of loathing and of shame. The distress of the people was such that multitudes were ready to follow a teacher into the wilderness, not for the sake of his words, but for the sake of a little bread. And from this oppression there was no appeal to remorse in the breast of the oppressor, or to the tribunal of a civilized world. There was no hope but in patriotic arms. Nor was the nation incapable of wielding them. The spirit of Gideon and of Judas Maccabeus glowed in it still. It cherished the constant hope of a great Deliverer. It was ready to rise. It rose, before long, with an energy which, though the issue was the destruction of Jerusalem, shook for a moment the adamantine throne of Rome. And even before the last great struggle more than one insurgent chief was able to lead his thousands into the wilderness. Everything, to a human apprehension, counselled an appeal to the strong hand: and strong hands and brave hearts were ready to answer to the call.

Nevertheless our Lord and His Apostles said not a word against the powers or institutions of that evil world. Their attitude towards them all was that of deep spiritual hostility and of entire political submission. The dominion of a foreign conqueror, the presence of his soldiery, the extortions of his tax-gatherers, the injustice of his judges, the iniquitous privileges of the conquering Roman, the iniquitous degradation of the conquered Jew,—all these, as well as slavery, are accepted with unquestioning resignation. The things which are Cæsar's are rendered unto Cæsar, though Cæsar is a Tiberius or a Nero. To endure patiently the dominion of those monsters, it has been truly said, was the honour of Christianity and the dishonour of mankind.

Had this implicit submission to political power not been preached by our Lord and His Apostles, and enforced by their example, the new religion must, humanly speaking, have perished in its birth. The religious movement would infallibly have become a political movement, as Protestantism did when preached by Wycliffe and Huss to an oppressed people. And

H

then the Roman would have come upon it and crushed it with his power. To support it against the Roman legions with legions of angels was not a part of the counsels of God.

St. Peter says, "Servants, be subject to your masters with all fear; not only to the good and gentle, but also to the froward. For this is thankworthy, if a man for conscience toward God endure grief, suffering wrongfully. For what glory is it, if, when ye be buffeted for your faults, ye shall take it patiently? but if, when ye do well, and suffer for it, ye take it patiently, this is acceptable with God. For even hereunto were ye called: because Christ also suffered for us, leaving us an example, that ye should follow His steps: who did no sin, neither was guile found in His mouth: who, when He was reviled, reviled not again; when He suffered, He threatened not; but committed Himself to Him that judgeth righteously: who His own self bare our sins in His own body on the tree, that we, being dead to sins, should live unto righteousness: by whose stripes ye were healed[c]." Is this an exhortation to modern society to establish, or suffer to be established, in the midst of Christianity, freedom, and equal law, an institution under which men are subject to the frowardness of masters, and under which they may be buffeted and made to suffer without regard to justice? If it be, it is equally an exhortation to modern society to embrace the whole circle of institutions which persecuted the Apostles and which crucified Christ.

"Submit yourselves," St. Peter has said just before,

[c] 1 Pet. ii. 18—24.

"to *every* ordinance of man for the Lord's sake: whether it be to the king, as supreme; or unto governors, as unto them that are sent by him for the punishment of evildoers, and for the praise of them that do well. For so is the will of God, that with well doing ye may put to silence the ignorance of foolish men: as free, and not using your liberty for a cloke of maliciousness, but as the servants of God. Honour all men. Love the brotherhood. Fear God. Honour the king."

St. Paul, like St. Peter, in several places commands slaves to obey their masters. But St. Paul, like St. Peter, also commands the masters themselves to obey a despotic Emperor and his arbitrary satraps. "Let every soul be subject unto the higher powers. For there is no power but of God; the powers that be are ordained of God. Whosoever therefore resisteth the power, resisteth the ordinance of God; and they that resist shall receive to themselves damnation." Channing says, "This passage was written in the time of Nero. It teaches passive obedience to despotism more strongly than any text teaches the lawfulness of slavery. Accordingly, it has been quoted for ages by the supporters of arbitrary power, and made the stronghold of tyranny. Did our fathers acquiesce in the most obvious interpretation of this text? Because the first Christians were taught to obey despotic rule, did our fathers feel as if Christianity had stripped men of their rights? Did they agree that tyranny was to be excused because forcible opposition to it was in most cases wrong? Did they argue that absolute power ceases to be unjust, because, as a general rule, it is the duty of subjects to obey? Did they infer that bad institutions ought to be perpetual, because the subversion of them by force will almost always inflict greater evil than it removes? No: they were wiser interpreters of God's Word. They believed that despotism was a wrong notwithstanding the general obligation upon its subjects to obey; and that whenever a whole people should so feel the wrong as to demand its removal, the time for removing it had fully come."

St. Paul knew what the "higher powers" were. He had suffered a life of persecution, stripes, imprisonments, and stonings at the hands of unbelievers. He was looking forward to a martyr's death at the same hands. Did he intend Christians to do these things to each other, or Christian Society to suffer these things to be done? Is there anything in the words of this or of any Apostle which would forbid Cromwell to protect the Protestants of Savoy by his intervention against their bloody persecutors, or which would have forbidden him, if necessary, to protect them with his arms?

"There is neither Jew nor Greek, there is neither bond nor free, there is neither male nor female: for ye are all one in Christ Jesus[d]." "Let every man abide in the same calling wherein he was called. Art thou called being a servant? care not for it: but if thou mayest be made free, use it rather. For he that is called in the Lord, being a servant, is the Lord's freeman: likewise also he that is called, being free, is Christ's servant. Ye are bought with a price; be not

[d] Gal. iii. 28.

ye the servants of men. Brethren, let every man, wherein he is called, therein abide with God[e]." These passages and the others in the New Testament relating to the established institutions of the time, inculcate on the disciples resignation to their earthly lot on spiritual grounds, and for the sake of a heavenly hope in which all earthly differences are swallowed up and lost. They do not inculcate social or political apathy; they do not pass, nor have they ever been held by men of common sense to pass, upon the Christian world a sentence of social or political despair. The faculties

[e] 1 Cor. vii. 20—24. Some commentators on this passage take "use it rather" (μᾶλλον χρῆσαι) as "use *slavery* rather"—"prefer to remain a slave." They say that the general sense of the passage requires this. Why so? The passage preaches tranquil acquiescence in a man's present state. But to exhort a man to acquiesce tranquilly in his present state is not to exhort him to refuse a better if it presents itself. The expression "care not for it" (μή σοι μελέτω) surely does not imply that slavery is in the opinion of the writer to be considered the better state. In εἰ καὶ δύνασαι, the καὶ may very well be taken, it is conceived, as merely lending emphasis to δύνασαι, and in fact as almost pleonastic. [Cf. Soph. Aj. 1106, δεινόν γ' εἶπας, εἰ καὶ ζῆς θανών.] 'If freedom *is* offered thee, without thy seeking, accept it.' So just before (ver. 13—15), a believing wife is enjoined not to leave an unbelieving husband if he be pleased to dwell with her; but it is added, "if the unbelieving depart, let him depart." The woman is not to break the bond: but she is not to cling to it if separation is offered her. When we look to the general tone and tenor of St. Paul's teaching on these matters, so far removed from enthusiasm and asceticism; when we consider that he knew the Old Testament, in which freedom is clearly treated as preferable to bondage; and when we remember that he had himself no scruple in asserting his privilege as a Roman citizen; it is difficult to believe that he can have enjoined a Christian Slave, when enfranchisement from a heathen master was offered him, to refuse the boon. It is not however of much consequence to the present argument which way the passage is taken; since St. Paul's precept, whatever it may be, is clearly given on spiritual, not on social or political, grounds.

for social improvement, and the desire to redress inequality and injustice, which God had given us, the Son of God did not take away. On the contrary, He and His Apostles increased those faculties and that desire a thousand-fold by the principles of mutual affection and duty which they instilled into the heart of man, and by the new force of self-devotion which they added to his moral powers.

    The relation of the Gospel to Slavery is well stated in a passage quoted by Channing from Wayland's "Elements of Moral Science:"—"The very course which the Gospel takes on this subject, seems to have been the only one that could have been taken in order to effect the universal abolition of Slavery. The Gospel was designed, not for one race or for one time, but for all races and for all times. It looked, not at the abolition of this form of evil for that age alone, but for its universal abolition. Hence the important object of its Author was to gain it a lodgment in every part of the known world; so that, by its universal diffusion among all classes of society, it might quietly and peacefully modify and subdue the evil passions of men, and thus, without violence, work a revolution in the whole mass of mankind. In this manner alone could its object, a universal moral revolution, have been accomplished. For if it had forbidden the *evil* instead of subverting the *principle*, if it had proclaimed the unlawfulness of Slavery, and taught slaves to *resist* the oppression of their masters, it would instantly have arrayed the two parties in deadly hostility throughout the civilized world; its announcement would have been the signal of servile war; and the very name of the Christian religion would have been forgotten amidst the agitations of universal bloodshed. The fact, under these circumstances, that the Gospel does not forbid Slavery, affords no reason to suppose that it does not mean to prohibit it; much less does it afford ground for belief that Jesus Christ intended *to authorize* it."

Channing himself says, "Slavery, in the age of the Apostle, had so penetrated society, was so intimately interwoven with it, and the materials of servile war were so abundant, that a religion, preaching freedom to the slave, would have shaken the social fabric to its foundation, and would have armed against itself the whole power of the State. Paul did not then assail the institution. He satisfied himself with spreading principles, which, however slowly, could not but work its destruction."

"Christianity," says Neander, "effected a change in the convictions of men from which a dissolution of the whole relation of slavery, though it could not be immediately accomplished, yet, by virtue of the consequences resulting from that change, was sure eventually to take place. This effect Christianity produced, first of all, by the facts to which it was a witness, and next by the ideas which, by means of these facts, it set in circulation. By Christ, the Saviour for all mankind, the differences among men resulting from sin were reconciled, by Him the original unity of the human race was restored. These facts must now operate in transforming the life of mankind. Masters as well as servants were obliged to acknowledge themselves the servants of sin, and must alike receive, as the free gift of God's grace, their deliverance from this common bondage—the *true, the highest freedom*. Servants and masters, if they had become believers, were brought together under the same bond of an heavenly union, destined for immortality; they became brethren in Christ in whom there is neither bond nor free, members of one body, baptized into one Spirit, heirs of the same heavenly inheritance. Servants were often the teachers of their masters in the Gospel, after having, first of all, in their lives and actions exhibited before them the loftiness of a divine life, which must be shewn forth even under the most painful of relations, and shine forth the more brightly by the contrast^f."

Not only did St. Paul and the other Apostles spread principles and ideas which were sure to work the destruction of Slavery and of the other political and social wrongs of which that corrupt and unjust world was full; but they embodied these principles and ideas in an institution, founded by their Lord, of which it may be said that though so little revolutionary in appearance that the most jealous tyranny might have received it into its bosom without suspicion, it exceeded in revolutionary efficacy any political force which has ever been seen in action among men. At the Supper of the Lord the conqueror was required, on his allegiance to Christianity, to partake in the holy meal with the conquered, the master with the slave; and this in memory of a Founder who had died the death of a slave upon the Cross, and who at the institution of the rite

[f] Church History, vol. i. p. 372. Eng. trans.

had performed the servile office of washing His disciples' feet.

In its social aspect as well as in other respects the Lord's Supper is the antitype and counterpart of the Passover, but in this as in its other aspects it is of far deeper and holier significance, and the symbol not of a family or national union, but of the union of mankind. It is difficult to imagine how any harsh distinctions between man and man could long maintain themselves against its equalizing and reconciling power. Nor has it failed to accomplish its object in this respect where it has been administered according to the intention of its founder. Where it has been administered in a way quite different from His intention, its efficacy could not be expected to be so great. During the feudal ages the relations between the lord and the serf were almost as unchristian as those between the modern slave-owner and his slave. But during the feudal ages the Supper of the Lord, as well as the worship of which it was the centre and the culmination, had lost its primitive character. It had ceased to be a communion in the full sense of the word, and had become a sort of magic rite administered to each member of the Church by the priest, the talisman and chief support of sacerdotal power.

In few countries were the people more oppressed and degraded by feudal tyranny down to the time of the Reformation than in Scotland. After the Reformation the lower classes were socially raised; and all classes have since become united in a remarkable degree, considering that the political institutions of the country remain aristocratic. It is reasonable to refer this in a great measure to the social character of the religious system. National education has no doubt done much; but national education has its source in the spirit of the national religion. Long after the Reformation the material condition of the poor in Scotland, owing to the poverty of the country, remained very wretched; and towards the end of the seventeenth century, when the Scottish peasantry had already played no mean part in the religious history of the world, Fletcher of Saltoun, a republican of the Classical school, proposed to redeem the Covenanters from their miserable, unprotected, and anxious state, and to restore them again to careless happiness under fatherly guidance, by making them prædial slaves.

If the Slave partook of the Lord's Supper, much more would he partake in all the other acts of Christian worship. Of course also he would fully share all the religious knowledge of his brethren, and everything that could enable them worthily to worship the God of Truth. He might, as Neander says, be the religious teacher of his master. And as his religious life was blended with that of his fellow-Christians, so his body would rest with theirs in death.

In America, as we have already had occasion to say, there appears, generally speaking, to be no religious communion between the Master and the Slave. The two classes do not belong in any practical sense to the same Church. They can scarcely be said even to unite in public worship; they do not join in family prayer, nor do they really partake together of the Supper of the Lord. The presence of a white man is indeed required by law at all the religious meetings of the negroes; but it is not for the purpose of taking part in their prayers [g].

More than this, it is only by putting names for things that the American Master and Slave can be said to be of the same religion. In some States the Master, for the better security of what is now called a divine institution, forbids the slave by law to be taught to read: so that the Bible is legally closed to him [h]. And even in the States where this legal prohibition does not exist, the state of public opinion and the almost total want of schools seem effectually to prevent the education of the great mass of the slaves [i]. And altogether, from their mode of life, and the debasing treatment to which they are subjected, their minds are too degraded to worship God in spirit and truth like those to whom a Christian education has been given. The result is that the worship of the negro in America is little more spiritual or rational than his worship in Africa. He still dances, and shouts to a fetish, though that fetish bears the name of the Christian's God.

Mr. Olmsted says, "In most of the large rice plantations which I have seen in this vicinity (South Caro-

[g] See Olmsted, Journeys and Explorations, vol. i. p. 45.

[h] In North Carolina, to teach a slave to read or write, or sell or give him any book (Bible not excepted) or pamphlet, is punished with thirty-nine lashes, or imprisonment, if the offender be a free negro; but if a white, then with a fine of 200 dollars. The reason for this law, assigned in its preamble, is, "that teaching slaves to read and write tends to dissatisfaction in their minds, and to produce insurrection and rebellion."—*Goodell's American Slave Code*, p. 299.

[i] Ibid., p. 301.

lina) there is a small chapel, which the negroes call their prayer-house. The owner of one of these told me that having furnished the prayer-house with seats having a back rail, his negroes petitioned him to remove it, because it did not leave them *room enough to pray.* It was explained to me that it is their custom, in social worship, to work themselves up to a great pitch of excitement, in which they yell and cry aloud, and finally, shriek and leap up, clapping their hands and dancing, as it is done in heathen festivals[k]." No doubt "heathen festival" is the right name.

The same writer has given a description of the religious exercises of negroes, which he witnessed himself in a chapel, not on a plantation, but in the city of New Orleans[l]. It is such that it could scarcely be transcribed without shocking the reader, and the religious state which it reveals has nothing, but the names which are hideously profaned, in common with the religion of Christians.

It seems that the American Slave-owners are so conscious of the connexion between truth and freedom that they sometimes repel with dread even the oral instruction of slaves in the truth. In South Carolina a Methodist clergyman had been chosen by his Church as a discreet and cautious man to preach to slaves. He was stopped by a remonstrance signed by more than three hundred and fifty of the leading planters and citizens. He pleaded that it was his intention to confine himself to verbal instruction. "Verbal instruction," replied the remonstrants, "will increase the de-

[k] Journeys and Explorations, vol. i. p. 259. [l] Ibid., p. 388.

sire of the black population to learn.... Open the Missionary sluice and the current will swell in its gradual onward advance. We thus expect a progressive system of improvement will be introduced, or will follow from the nature and force of circumstances which, if not checked, (though it may be shrouded in sophistry and disguise,) will ultimately revolutionize our civil institutions." The missionary withdrew, and the local newspaper in announcing his withdrawal stated that the great body of the people were manifestly opposed to the religious instruction of their slaves, even if it were only given orally [m].

And when, in despite of the difficulties thrown in the way, some religious knowledge has been obtained by the negroes, the enjoyment of it seems to be not very secure. Twenty-four coloured men, most of them apparently free, were found assembling privately in the evening at Washington, and were lodged in the watch-house. When they were examined before a magistrate, no evidence was offered, nor does it appear to have been even suggested, that they were meeting for any criminal purpose. On searching their persons, there were found a Bible, a volume of Seneca's "Morals," "Life in Earnest," the printed constitution of a Society the object of which was stated to be to relieve the sick and bury the dead, and a subscription paper to purchase the freedom of a slave whom her master was willing to sell at a certain price. One of the prisoners, a slave, was ordered to be flogged; four

[m] Olmsted, Journeys and Explorations, vol. ii. p. 214.

others, called in the papers free men, were sent to the workhouse: and the rest, on paying costs and fines amounting to one hunded and eleven dollars, were set at liberty [n].

It is not wonderful that a gross and delirious superstition should fail to produce the effect of pure Christianity on the morals of the negroes. Mr. Olmsted gives us strong evidence of their licentiousness; and notably of the licentiousness of those among them who are members of Churches and make professions of religion [o]. But indeed the legal sanctity of marriage is so essential a safeguard of morality in Christian countries, that we should expect sinister consequences to flow from its withdrawal. In the South the marriage of a slave is, before the law and in the eyes of his master, as the cohabitation of beasts. The State thus preaches disregard of morality to the negro, and the master enforces the preaching of the State by practices from which it was part of the mission of Christianity to purge the world [p].

Let the Masters and the Slaves in America become

---

[n] Olmsted, Journeys and Explorations, vol. i. p. 36. If we are told, by way of apology for the intellectual and religious condition of the negro slave, that the intellectual and religious condition of the English peasant and his religious relations to the upper classes are unsatisfactory, the answer is that they are acknowledged to be unsatisfactory, and that since the revival of a religious spirit in the nation a good deal has been done to amend them, as a multitude of schools and a number of new churches with free sittings evince.

[o] Journey in the Back Country, p. 113.

[p] Olmsted, Journeys and Explorations, vol. ii. p. 229. When the Abolitionists are charged with producing the Slave-owner's cruelty by their alarming denunciations, they may reasonably ask whether they are also to be charged with producing his lust.

really fellow-Christians: let them become in a true sense one Church: let them share the same Christian education: let them read the same Bible: let them partake of the Communion together: and it will then be seen whether the relation between fellow-Christians is really compatible with the relation between Master and Slave.

That there are very great difficulties in the way of a religious as well as of a social fusion between the negroes and the whites, no reasonable man would deny. But this shews that the position into which the piratical cupidity of the whites has brought the two races is an awkward one; not that it was sanctioned by St. Paul. As things are at present, the plea that Slavery is a great blessing as a missionary agency, and as a mode of bringing the African heathen within the fold of the Church, can scarcely be maintained. Montesquieu has some remarks on the notion that "religion gives those who profess it the right of making slaves of those who do not, in order the better to labour for its propagation." "It was this notion," he says, "which encouraged the destroyers of America in their crimes. It was on this idea that they founded the right of making all those nations slaves; for these brigands, who were determined to be both brigands and Christians, were very devout."

It is to be borne in mind that the Apostle, who bids slaves obey their masters and be content with their lot for the sake of their Lord's religion and in the assurance of a higher freedom, also teaches masters to observe justice and equity towards their slaves. "Masters, give unto your servants that which is just and equal: knowing that ye also have a Master in Heaven." Is "that which is just and equal" given to a slave when he is forbidden to learn to read, when he is denied legal marriage, when he is separated by force from his wife and children, when his evidence is refused in a court of law, when he is made by custom, though not by law, the victim of a penal code under which a master who kills a slave goes unpunished, while a slave who kills a master may be burned alive at a slow fire?

No doubt many American masters are better than the system. Many Roman masters were better than the system. But is it possible to believe that the system is one which, when carried on by Christians against Christians, can be said to have had its prototype in the relations between a Christian master, in Apostolic times, and his slave, or to be sanctioned by the teaching of the Apostles?

In a religious community so bound together in life and death as that of the early Christians, the relation between Master and Slave, though it was not formally dissolved, must have been completely transfigured, and virtually exchanged for a relation between brethren in Christ. The clearest proof of this is found in that very Epistle of St. Paul to Philemon which those who defend Slavery on Scriptural grounds regard as their sheet anchor in the argument. St. Paul sends back the fugitive slave Onesimus to his master Philemon. Therefore, we are told, slavery and fugitive slave laws have received the sanction of St. Paul. This it seems is so plain, that the refusal of the other party to acknowledge it is a signal instance of the manner in which they blind themselves to the clearest teachings of Scripture, or pervert its precepts in the interest of a spurious humanity. It is very true that St. Paul sends back a fugitive slave to his Master. But does he send him back *as a slave?* The best answer to the argument drawn from the Epistle to Philemon is the simple repetition of the words of that Epistle: "I beseech thee for my son Onesimus, whom I have begotten in my bonds: which in time past was to thee unprofitable, but now profitable to thee and to me: whom I have sent again: thou therefore receive him, that is, mine own bowels: whom I would have retained with me, that in thy stead he might have ministered unto me in the bonds of the Gospel: but without thy mind would I do nothing; that thy benefit should not be as it were of necessity, but willingly. For perhaps he therefore departed for a season, that thou shouldest receive him for ever; not now as a servant, but above a servant, a brother beloved, specially to me, but how much more unto thee, both in the flesh, and in the Lord? If thou count me therefore a partner, receive him as myself. If he hath wronged thee, or oweth thee aught, put that on mine account. I Paul have written it with mine own hand, I will repay it: albeit I do not say to thee how thou owest unto me even thine own self besides[q]."

Onesimus, then, is not sent back as a slave, but as one above a servant, a brother beloved.

[q] Phil. v. 10—19.

When fugitive slaves in America are sent back to their masters with such letters as that of St. Paul to Philemon, and treated as St. Paul expects Onesimus to be treated on their return, American slavery will have some claim to be regarded as a Scriptural institution. But in that case it will also be near its end. For such a feeling as the writer of the Epistle supposes to exist in the hearts of Christians as to their relations with each other, though it would not prevent a Christian slave from remaining in the service of his master, would certainly prevent a Christian master from continuing to hold his fellow Christian as a slave.

St. Paul must have known what Slavery under the Roman Empire was. He must have known that it was a vast reign not only of abominable cruelty, but of still more abominable lust. He must have known that it was fed to a great extent by the man-stealing which he classes with murder and parricide. He must have known the deadly effects which it produced on the character of the Slave-owner, to whose unbridled passions human beings of both sexes were subjected without limit or redress[r]. He must have known that this was the real "cancer" which was eating into the vitals of morality and drawing society to its ruin. It would have been strange therefore if he had selected

[r] Let it be observed that in those days there were no Abolitionists to disturb, by their fanatical attacks, the kindly relations between the Slave and his Master, or to mar the harmonious working of the institution. The world saw, by a fair and decisive experiment, what it was to give man a despotic and uncontrolled power over man. That tyranny is mildest when it is unchecked and undenounced is a theory flattering to human nature, but not verified by the experience of history.

this among all the political and social institutions of the time as the object of a partisanship which neither he nor any of his fellow Apostles have in any other case betrayed.

The philosophic theory as to ineradicable differences of race, on which Slavery is now founded by its defenders, is directly contradicted by the New Testament, for St. Paul says that "God has made of one blood all nations of men, for to dwell on all the face of the earth[s]." In conformity with this declaration, St. Paul and his fellow Apostles proceeded to found a Church which was to embrace all nations. It is difficult to imagine a race of beings fit to apprehend the sublimest doctrines of Christianity, to live by the Christian rule, and to hold office in the Christian Church, yet not fit to be masters of their own persons, to enjoy the rights of husbands and of fathers, to receive the elements of education, or give evidence in a court of justice.

The only refuge for those who defend Slavery on grounds of race, if they do not wish to contradict St. Paul, seems to be to go the full length of saying that the negroes are not "a nation of *men*." And to this suggestion the Slave-owner, as we have hinted before, has given and daily gives a conclusive answer by the practices which fill the country with a mixed race.

Nor would it be easy to produce from the New Testament anything which could give colour to the view that a class of free labourers is the fungus and cancer of civilized life, and that the community is immeasurably benefited when the labourer is made a slave. For

[s] Acts xvii. 26.

it was from this diseased and pestilential element of society, as the advocates of slavery hold it to be, that the Apostles themselves were chosen. The founder of Christianity Himself wore the form of a carpenter's son. St. Paul wrought as a tent-maker. He "laboured working with his own hands." And he laid upon his followers in broad terms, and without making any exception, the injunction "that if any would not work neither should he eat." Judging from his language, we should say that if there was any particular form of society which the Apostle desired to found, it was not one in which the true citizen should be exempt from labour, but one in which labour should be the lot of all, and all should contribute to the common store.

Feudalism tried to prove that the Apostles were gentlemen by birth, entitled to bear coats of arms. They would have to undergo some historical transformation of a similar kind to make them fit founders of the religion professed by the Slave-owning aristocracy of the South.

"Would you do a benefit to the horse or the ox by giving him a cultivated understanding or fine feelings? So far as the *mere labourer* has the pride, the knowledge, or the aspirations of a free man, he is unfitted for his situation, and must doubly feel its infelicity. If there are sordid, servile, and laborious offices to be performed, is it not better that there should be sordid, servile, and laborious beings to perform them?" Such is the opinion of Chancellor Harper, put forth in his address to the South Carolina Institute. Was it the opinion of a Master who washed His disciples' feet?

It is difficult to understand how people who hold these sentiments can even use, without a sense of unfitness, the common language of Christianity. Such phrases as "Whosoever will be chief among you, let him be your servant," must seem to them to denote something sordid and degrading.

"It is by the existence of slavery," says another Southern writer, "exempting so large a portion of our citizens from labour, that we have leisure for intellectual pursuits." But there is something in the spirit of the Gospel which, whether rightly or wrongly understood, has led Christianity, instead of cherishing an exclusive intellectual order, to educate the poor; and to draw forth, by all the means in its power, the intellectual gifts of that class for the highest service of the community. Great systems of education, the direct offspring of Christianity, and a multitude of Christian foundations for the purpose of education, bear witness to the fact. Nor do the comparative fruits of the two systems, so far as they have been tried, condemn the common practice of the Christian world. On the contrary, the principle that all orders are "members one of another" seems, when applied to education, to act more favourably on the intellect even of the higher class than the opposite principle. "From the banks of the Mississippi to the banks of the James," says a traveller in the South, "I did not (that I remember) see, except perhaps in one or two towns, a thermometer, nor a book of Shakspeare, nor a pianoforte or sheet of music; nor the light of a carcel or other good centre table or reading-lamp, nor an engraving or copy of any kind of a work of art of the slightest merit." "I am not speaking," he adds, "of what are commonly called 'poor whites;' a large majority of all these houses were the residences of shareholders, a considerable proportion cotton-planters [t]." Some of the compositions which are the fruits of the "intellectual leisure" purchased by the hopeless degradation of the labouring class are before us. They are among the most barbarous ever produced by civilized man. They seem moreover to turn mainly on one subject. The presence of a great social wrong absorbs such intellect as the community has in the work of its justification. It does not leave the real leisure and the serenity of mind which philosophy, science, and poetry demand.

New England has taken the course sanctioned by Christendom and condemned by the Slaver. Like Scotland, or even more than Scotland, she has made a system of popular education the basis of her Commonwealth, and established throughout her territory the free schools which, above all other free institutions, the South, as we have seen, repudiates and abhors. The result of this is that intelligence is generally diffused among the people, and that the great writers of England have a second and an ample Empire in the North. The highest fruits of intellect are everywhere long in ripening; and this must especially be the case in a nation of which a large part consists of immigrants, intent on obtaining the means of subsistence, and the energies of which are to a great extent absorbed in providing the material basis of civilization and reclaiming a vast ex-

[t] Journeys and Explorations, vol. ii. p. 285.

panse of virgin land. Under such circumstances, the love of utility must be expected to predominate over that of beauty, practical invention over pure science, practical discussion over the pursuit of theoretic truth. Yet the North has already produced writers in different departments who take a high place in literature, and who may fairly be regarded as the earnest of still better things to come. Men of intellect are very apt, from their natural fastidiousness, to dislike Equality; yet if they look over history they will find that Equality has been their best friend.

There is nothing, the prevalence of which in a community is more fatal to high intellect, than gross luxury. And there can be no doubt that in a modern Slave State gross luxury prevails in the highest degree. The ancient Slave States at the time of their intellectual greatness were comparatively free from luxury, at least of the grosser kind.

In fact, the character to which the Slave-owners aspire seems to be not so much that of the Christian, with its charity and humility, or even that of the intellectual Greek, as that of the ancient Roman. "The relations between the North and the South," says a Southern organ, "are very analogous to those which subsisted between Greece and the Roman Empire, after the subjugation of Achaia by the Consul Mummius. The dignity and energy of the Roman character, conspicuous in war and politics, were not easily toned and adjusted to the arts of industry and literature. The degenerate and pliant Greeks, on the contrary, excelled in the handicraft and polite professions. We learn from the vigorous invective of Juvenal, that they were the most useful and capable of servants, whether as pimps or professors of rhetoric. Obsequious, dexterous, and ready, the versatile Greeks monopolized the business of teaching, publishing, and manufacturing in the Roman Empire, allowing their masters ample leisure for the service of the State, in the Senate or in the field." In confirmation of this historical theory it may be remarked that the Romans of the Southern States, like those of the Capitol, sprang from an asylum. One who was much concerned in the foundation of Virginia said of that Colony, that "the number of felons and vagabonds transported did bring such evil characters on the place, that some did choose to be hanged ere they would go there, *and were.*"

It is true that the planters also claim a reputation for chivalry; and chivalry, no doubt, has its root deep in Christianity. But we must beg leave to add that a chivalry which exercises uncontrolled tyranny over defenceless victims, which flogs women naked, which buys and sells them as the wretched victims of brutal lust, which breeds human beings like cattle, which tears husbands from their wives and children from their mothers, which stands by and exults or moralizes while men are burned alive at slow fires, is a chivalry such as the Christian world has not yet seen. The type of character which it tends to produce may be higher than that of St. Louis, Edward I., and Bayard, but it certainly is not the same.

We have said that the founders of Christianity, when they preached political resignation as necessary for the time, did not pass on mankind a sentence of political despair. They submitted to the powers of an evil world, but they nevertheless did, and meant to do, that by which those powers would be destroyed. They bade the slave remain a slave, but it was in order that he might not imperil the sacred deposit of Christian principle which bore with it the redemption of the slave for ever. The kingdom of Christ was not of this world, but nevertheless its liegemen looked forward to the day when "the kingdoms of this world should become the kingdoms of our Lord and His Christ, and that He should reign for ever and ever."

Therefore the Church, whenever she has been herself, and whenever she has acted in the spirit of her Founder, has laboured, not by inciting revolution, but by inculcating social duty and kindling social affection, to do away with all unjust and harsh distinctions between man and man, to diffuse the principles of fraternity and equality in their true sense through the world, and to make each community a community indeed. Therefore she has instinctively and steadily insisted on the education of the poor. Therefore she has steadily assailed slavery and caste, and feudal serfdom, and all such barriers as prevented the different classes of men in Christian nations from becoming members one of another. The brotherhood of man, in short, is the idea which Christianity in its social phase has been always striving to realize, and the progress of which constitutes the social history of Christendom. With what difficulties this idea has struggled; how it has been marred by revolutionary violence, as well as impeded by reactionary selfishness; to what chimerical hopes, to what wild schemes, to what calamitous disappointments, to what desperate conflicts, it has given birth; how often, being misunderstood and misapplied, it has brought not peace on earth but a sword,—it is needless here to rehearse. Such miscarriages, such delay, could not be averted unless the nature of man was to be changed, or the effort by which his character is formed, and which appears to be the law of his being, was to be superseded by the fiat of Omnipotence. Countless ages have no doubt yet to run before the idea is realized and the hope fulfilled. Still, as we look back over the range of past history, we can see beyond doubt that it is towards this goal that Christianity as a social principle has been always tending and still tends.

No sooner did the new religion gain power in the world, than the slave law, and the slave system of the Empire, began to be undermined by its influence. In unconscious alliance with Stoicism, to which among all the ancient systems of Philosophy it had the most affinity, Christianity broke in upon the despotism of the Master, as well as upon the despotism of the Father and the Husband. The right of life and death over the Slave was transferred from his owner to the magistrate. The right of correction was placed under humane limitations, which the magistrate was directed to maintain. All the restrictions on the enfranchisement of Slaves were swept away. The first Christian Emperor recognised enfranchisement as a religious act, and established the practice of performing it in the Church before the Bishop, and in the presence of the congregation. The liberties of the freedman were at the same time cleared of all odious and injurious restrictions. This remained the policy of the Christian Empire. The Code of Justinian, the great monument of Imperial jurisprudence, is highly favourable to enfranchisement, and that on religious grounds.

The facility of enfranchisement, and the prospect of enlarging that facility, would conspire with political prudence to prevent Christianity from coming into direct collision with Roman slavery. Hope was not denied to the Roman slave. But hope is denied, or almost denied, to the American slave. In most of the Southern States the law withholds the power of enfranchisement from the master, against whose benevolence and generosity it seems the State is more concerned to guard, than against his cruelty and lust. A slave can be emancipated only by the authority of the Legislature or by a Court of Law, and upon special cause shewn; and further, the condition of a Negro when emancipated is such, as to make freedom at once a very qualified and a very precarious boon. The free Negro is still to a great extent excluded from the rights of a citizen and a man. His evidence is not received against a white man[u]; the law does not secure to him the safeguard of a trial by a jury of his peers; he has no vote or voice in framing the laws by which he is governed, and degrading restrictions are imposed even

[u] "It is an inflexible and universal rule of slave-law, founded in one or two States upon usage, in others sanctioned by express legislation, that the testimony of a coloured person, whether bond or free, cannot be received against a white person."—*Wheeler's Law of Slavery,* quoted by *Goodell,* p. 279.

upon his religious worship. He is liable to be brought back into slavery in many ways,—among others, by being married to a slave; and if his freedom is challenged, he must bring white witnesses to prove himself free[x]. By the Roman Law the presumption was in favour of freedom, and under the Empire, freedmen not only enjoyed full liberty, but from their industry and pliancy often engrossed too much power in the State.

But the Roman world was doomed; and it was doomed partly because the character of the upper classes had been deeply and incurably corrupted by the possession of a multitude of slaves. The feudal age succeeded; the barbarian conqueror took the place of the Roman master, and a new phase of slavery appeared. Immediately Christianity recommenced its work of alleviation and enfranchisement. The codes of laws framed for the new lords of Europe under the influence of the Clergy, shew the same desire as those of the Christian Emperors, to break in upon the despotism of the Master, and assure personal rights to the Slave. The laws of the Lombards, for instance, protected the Serf against an unjust or too rigorous master; they set free the husband of a female slave who had been seduced by her owner; they assured the protection of the Churches to slaves who had taken refuge there, and regulated the penalties to be inflicted for their faults, instead of leaving them subject to an arbitrary will[y]. In England the Clergy secured for the Slave rest on the Sun-

---

[x] Goodell's American Slave Code, pt. iii. ch. i.
[y] Sismondi, Rep. Ital., vol. i. p. 74.

day, and liberty either to rest or work for himself on a number of holydays. They exhorted their flocks to leave the savings and earnings of the prædial slave untouched. They constantly freed the slaves who came into their own possession. They exhorted the laity to do the same, and what living covetousness refused, they often wrung from deathbed penitence. This they did constantly and effectually during the early part of the Middle Ages, while the Church was still to a great extent in a missionary state, and had not yet been turned into an establishment allied with political power. Afterwards no doubt a change came over the spirit of the Clergy in this, as well as in other respects. The Church became an Estate and a part of the feudal system. Her Bishops became Spiritual Lords. And these Spiritual Lords in the time of Richard II. voted with the Temporal Lords, for the repudiation of the King's promise of enfranchisement to the villains, and the last serfs who remained in existence were found on the estates of the Church.

Twice vanquished, in the shape of Ancient Slavery and in the shape of Feudal Serfdom, the enemy rose again in the shape of Negro Slavery, the offspring not of Roman or Barbarian Conquest, but of commercial avarice and cruelty. And again Christianity returned to the struggle against the barrier thus a third time reared by tyranny and cupidity in the path of her great social hope and mission, the brotherhood of Man. By the mouth of Clarkson and Wilberforce she demanded and obtained of a Christian nation the emancipation of the Slaves in the West Indies. And if in the case of American Slavery, the upper classes of this country, from political considerations, have shewn a change of feeling, and the Clergy of the Established Church have gone with the upper classes, the Free Churches, more unbiassed organs of Christianity, have almost universally kept the faith.

If, then, we look to the records of Christianity in the Bible, we find no sanction for American Slavery there. If we look to the history of Christendom, we find the propagators and champions of the faith assailing Slavery under different forms and in different ages, without concert, yet with a unanimity which would surely be strange if Christianity and Slavery were not the natural enemies of each other.

On the other side of the Atlantic two communities are now grappling in deadly conflict. The principle of one of them is Free Labour, while that of the other is Slavery; and few can doubt that this is the root of their antagonism, whatever may be the immediate cause of the present war.

It can hardly be denied that the community of New England, of which Free Labour is the principle, was founded under the auspices of Christianity, though it may have been Christianity of an austere and narrow kind, such as persecution produces in peasant hearts. The avowed object of the settlement was "the glory of God and the advancement of the Christian faith;" and one of the fathers of the Colony said, "It concerneth New England to remember that they were originally a plantation religious, not a plantation of trade. If any man among us make religion as twelve, and the world as thirteen, such an one hath not the spirit of a true New Englandman." The settlers at first, like the Early Church, had all things in common, till the natural desire of separate property arose, and in this, as in other respects, the little religious community became a nation. The primary germ of the Puritan settlement has, of course, been overlaid by a vast alien immigration; the original character of the people has to a great extent disappeared under the vast growth of the commercial element; and other things have taken place which would make it difficult for one of the Pilgrim Fathers, if he could return to life, to recognise the offspring of his "religious plantation" in the America of the present day. Still the great Christian idea so far survives that it remains the fundamental principle of the community to treat all men as equally entitled to the full benefit of the social union, and to make the State a brotherhood of which all are equally recognised as members. And the destinies of a community of which this can be said, whatever may be its defects, its errors, or its misfortunes, cannot cease to be an object of interest to Christendom.

Virginia and the Confederate States, on the other hand, of which Slavery is declared to be the fundamental principle, were assuredly not founded under the auspices of Christianity. They were founded by mere commercial adventurers of the very lowest kind. They were fostered by that darker Power which waits on the beneficent genius of commerce, and of which slave-trading Bristol was then the chosen seat. This power has been worshipped in all ages with human misery and blood. It has led men in all ages to reduce their fellow men to slavery for their own profit. It leads men now to put their own children under the lash of the overseer. Nor does the Slave Power fail, in its extremity, to receive the sympathy of the element from which it is sprung. The heart of capitalist tyranny everywhere is with that supreme tyranny of capital which makes its victims slaves. Feudalism, too, knows its own, and feels its affinity to a system under which, as in the times of serfdom, the labourer is under the absolute dominion of the lord.

Christian England tampered with Slavery for wealth. She has paid the penalty of her offence in the depraving influence of the West Indian slave-owners on the character and manners of this nation, in the heavy sum which, when the hour of remorse arrived, was given to purchase Emancipation, and in the burden and expense of holding a number of useless dependencies in the West Indies; a burden and expense which will probably be greatly increased if a great Slave Power is established on the neighbouring shore. The Christian States of North America have tampered with Slavery for Empire and for the pride of a great Confederacy; and they have paid the penalty, first in the poison which the domination of the Slave-owner has spread through their political and social system, and secondly, in this dreadful and disastrous war.

Printed by Messrs. Parker, Cornmarket, Oxford.

By the same Author.

Second Edition, Post 8vo., cloth lettered, price 5s.
Irish History and Irish Character.

Uniform with the above, price 6s.
The Empire.
A Series of Letters published in "The Daily News," 1862, 1863.

8vo., cloth, price 4s.
Three Lectures on Modern History,
delivered in Oxford, 1859-61.

I., II. On the Study of History.
III. On some supposed consequences of the Doctrine of Historical Progress.

With A LETTER to the "Daily News" defending the principles maintained in the Lectures against the "Westminster Review."

8vo., price 1s.
The Foundation of the American Colonies.
A Lecture delivered before the University of Oxford, June 12, 1860.

OXFORD AND LONDON: JOHN HENRY AND JAMES PARKER.

Oxford Professorial Lectures,
Recently published.

Three Lectures on Taxation,
ESPECIALLY THAT OF LAND, delivered at Oxford, in the Year 1860. By CHARLES NEATE, M.A., Fellow of Oriel; Professor of Political Economy in the University of Oxford. 8vo., price 2s.

By the same Author.
Two Lectures on Trades Unions,
Delivered in the University of Oxford in the year 1861. 8vo., price 1s. 6d.

On the Principle of Non-Intervention.
A Lecture delivered in the Hall of All Souls' College. By MOUNTAGUE BERNARD, M.A., Chichele Professor of International Law and Diplomacy in the University of Oxford. 8vo., price 1s.

By the same Author.
Two Lectures on the Present American War.
November, 1861. 8vo., sewed, price 2s.

Notes on some Questions Suggested by the Case of the "Trent." 8vo., price 1s.

Three Vols., Fcap. 8vo., with Illustrations, cloth, 15s.
Recommended by the Examiners in the School of Modern History at Oxford.
The Annals of England;
AN EPITOME OF ENGLISH HISTORY, From Contemporary Writers, the Rolls of Parliament, and other Public Records.

Vol. I. From the Roman Era to the Death of Richard II.
Vol. II. From the Accession of the House of Lancaster to Charles I.
Vol. III. From the Commonwealth to the Death of Queen Anne.

OXFORD AND LONDON: JOHN HENRY AND JAMES PARKER.

www.ingramcontent.com/pod-product-compliance
Lightning Source LLC
Chambersburg PA
CBHW020100170426
43199CB00009B/352